EMPLOYMENT LAW IN THE NHS

Viv Du-Feu, LLB, FIPM
Partner — Eversheds, Cardiff

Owen Warnock, MA (Cantab)
Partner — Eversheds, Norwich

Cavendish
Publishing
Limited

First published in Great Britain 1995 by Cavendish Publishing Limited, The Glass House, Wharton Street, London, WC1X 9PX. Telephone: 0171-278 8000   Facsimile: 0171-278 8080

British Library Cataloguing in Publication Data

Du-Feu, V
Employment Law in the NHS
I. Title II. Series
344.1041251

ISBN 1-85941-016-2

Printed and bound in Great Britain

ACKNOWLEDGEMENTS

The authors wish to acknowledge the help and support in the preparation of this text from their colleagues Simon Loy, Helen Mortlock, Elisabeth Jenkins and Richard Lowe.

CONTENTS

1 TERMS AND CONDITIONS OF EMPLOYMENT 1
Introduction – NHS terms of employment 1
Advantages of Whitley 1
Disadvantages of Whitley 2
The move away from common terms 2
Written particulars of employment 3
The basic legal requirements 3
Layout 4
Changeover from the old rules to the new rules 7
Changes to terms and conditions 7
Distinction between the written particulars
and the contract of employment 7
Signature to written particulars 9
Right to itemised pay statement 9

2 SPECIAL HEALTH SERVICE TERMS OF EMPLOYMENT 11
Sick pay 11
Continuity of employment 12
Redundancy 13
Premature retirement 15
Protection of earnings 16
Confidentiality and relations within the public media 17
Introduction 17
Patient information 18
The affairs of the employer 19

3 MATERNITY RIGHTS 21
Historical background 21
The detail 22
Statutory maternity leave 22
Whitley Council maternity rights 23
Compulsory maternity leave 25
Traps arising from discrepancies between statutory 14
week maternity leave and the Whitley Council rights 25
Publish a maternity policy 26
What job is the employee entitled to return to? 26
What if it is not practicable for the employer to
take the employee back? 27
Rights after return to work 28
Enforcement of maternity rights and protection
against dismissal 28
Pay during maternity and the law of sex discrimination 31
Maternity rights and fixed term contracts 31
Suspension on health and safety grounds 32

Summary of hazards, risks and ways of avoiding them	34
Return to work part-time after maternity	36
Maternity pay	36
4 DISCRIMINATION	39
Introduction	39
Definition	40
Direct discrimination	40
Indirect discrimination	40
Employers' liability	42
The employer's statutory defence	42
Pre-employment discrimination	43
Recruitment	43
Advertising	43
Application forms	45
Criteria for shortlisting	45
Interviews	46
Genuine occupational qualifications	46
GOQs (sex)	47
GOQs (race and sex)	49
GOQ (race only)	49
Discrimination during employment	50
Promotion	50
Restrictions on transfer	51
Restrictions on training	51
Exceptions for positive encouragement and training	51
Facilities and benefits	52
Mobility clauses	52
Dismissal	53
Constructive dismissal	53
Victimisation	54
Part-time employees	55
Homosexuality	56
Disability	58
Disabled Persons (Registration) Regulations 1945	60
Disabled Persons (Employment) Act 1944	60
Code of practice	61
Harassment	61
Questionnaire procedure	62
Remedies for discrimination and harassment	63
Injury to feelings award	64
Interest	64

CONTENTS

5   EQUAL PAY   65
     Aims of the governing legislation   65
     Scope of the equal pay legislation   65
     Significance of EU law   66
     The definition of 'pay'   67
     Types of claims under the Equal Pay Act   67
     Occupational Pension Schemes   68
     Choice of Comparator for the purposes of making
            a claim under the Equal Pay Act   68
     Choosing counterparts where male and female employees
            are employed on the same terms doing the same work   69
     Grounds for making a claim under the Equal Pay Act   70
     Defences to a claim made under the Equal Pay Act   71
            The genuine material factor defence   71
     Pay structures developed through collective bargaining   72
     Material factor – partial defence   73
     Further defences in equal value cases   73
     Determining whether the work of the claimant and the
            comparator is of equal value   74
     Designing contracts of employment to meet
            employees' specific needs   74
     Time limits for making a claim   75
     Cost to the employer of losing a claim   75
     No contracting out of the Equal Pay Act provisions   76
     Proactive claim prevention by the employer   76

6   MARKET TESTING – THE ACQUIRED RIGHTS DIRECTIVE
     77/187 AND THE TRANSFER OF UNDERTAKINGS
     (PROTECTION OF EMPLOYMENT) REGULATIONS 1981   79
     The Directive and TUPE   79
     The importance of the Directive and TUPE to the health sector   79
     The importance of the Directive   80
     The essential features of the Directive and TUPE as far as
            the health sector is concerned   80
     The transfer of an 'undertaking'   81
     Conclusion   83
     The 'transfer' of the undertaking   84
     Future development – a revised Directive   86
     Conclusion   87
     Steps which may be taken to clarify the position
            before the event   88
     Identifying which employees will transfer   89
     Employees who transfer from a regional or district health
            authority to an NHS Trust   91

The consequences if the Directive and TUPE do apply   91
The obligation to inform and consult   92
    To whom the obligations are owed   92
    By whom the obligations are owed   93
    Information which must be given   94
    The duty to consult   94
    When to start the process of information
       (and consultation)   94
    The defence if these obligations are not complied with   95
    The sanction for failing to comply with the duties to
       inform and consult   96
The automatic transfer of the contract of employment   96
    The obligations and rights transferred   97
    The defence available to the employer   97
    Dismissals prior to the transfer which are unconnected
       with the transfer   98
    What precisely does transfer   98
    Pension rights   99
    Restrictive covenants   100
    Share option/profit share/bonus scheme   101
    To what extent can the terms and conditions of
       employment of transferred employees be changed   101
The sharing of liability between transferor and transferee   102
The right of the employee to object to the automatic transfer
    of his employment contract to the transferee   103

7   DISMISSAL – SPECIAL FEATURES IN THE
    HEALTH SERVICE   105
    Introduction – the law of unfair dismissal   105
    Health service dismissal procedures   108
    Recurrent problems with health service dismissals   108
       Problem area 1 – lack of management action   108
       Problem area 2 – unwieldy procedures   109
       Problem area 3 – delay   109
       Problem area 4 – precedents   110
       Problem area 5 – publicity   110
       Summary on problem areas   112
    Dismissal for ill health and absence control   112
    Trade union representation and recognition   113
    Special advantages enjoyed by the health service in
       relation to dismissal   114

8   SPECIAL PROCEDURES FOR DISCIPLINING AND DISMISSING
     CONSULTANTS   115
     Introduction   115
     What procedures are there for handling doctors'
          disciplinary issues?   116
          Personal misconduct   116
          Professional misconduct/incompetence   116
          Professional misconduct/incompetence arising
               from mental health or physical disability   117
          Appeals against dismissal   117
     How do I decide into which category to place the
          misconduct/incompetence in order to invoke the
          correct procedure?   118
          What is personal misconduct?   118
          What is professional misconduct?   118
          What is professional incompetence?   119
          Are there any special considerations that apply when
               operating local procedures in relation to doctors who
               allegedly have personally misconducted themselves? 119
     The professional review machinery HC (90) (9) Annex D   120
          When is the professional review machinery appropriate? 120
          Who can initiate the review?   120
          What form does the review take?   121
          What records are kept of the panel meetings?   121
          Is a complainant exposed to defamation proceedings? 121
          When is the intermediate procedure appropriate?   122
          Who can initiate the procedure?   122
          If the medical director is satisfied that it is appropriate to
               deal with the allegation under the intermediate procedure,
               what form does the intermediate procedure take? 122
          What form does the assessment take?   122
          What right do the practitioners have during
               the assessment?   123
          What are the assessors required to do?   123
          Who decides whether disciplinary action will be taken? 123
          How should any appeal against disciplinary
               action be handled?   124
     Serious cases of professional misconduct or incompetence
          HC (90) (9) Annex B   124
          When is this procedure appropriate?   124
          What power is there to suspend?   124
          What time limits are imposed?   124

CONTENTS

What form does a preliminary investigation take? 125
Does there always have to be an enquiry by an
    investigatory panel? 125
If an enquiry is held what form does it take? 126
What form does the enquiry's report take? 126
Who takes any decision in relation to dismissal? 126
Appeal to the Secretary of State under paragraph 190 of the
    Medical and Dental Whitley Council
    (HC (90) (9) Annex C) 127
What are the qualifying conditions that a practitioner
    must fulfil in order to be able to appeal to the
    Secretary of State? 127
What happens in cases of mixed personal/professional
    competence? 128
When must the notice be served to exercise this right of appeal? 128
How is the appeal panel constituted? 129
What recommendation does the professional
    committee make? 129
Is the practitioner entitled to pay throughout
    the proceedings? 129

9   NOTICE OF TERMINATION, FIXED TERM CONTRACTS AND
    PAY IN LIEU OF NOTICE 131
Ordinary contracts 131
Fixed term and purpose or event contracts 132
What is the value of fixed term, purpose or event contracts? 133
Termination in breach of contract 134
What is the measure of loss? 135
Compensation for benefits in kind 137
Tax on large termination payments 137
The NHSME ready reckoner 138

10   ACHIEVING CHANGE TO TERMS OF EMPLOYMENT 139
Introduction 139
Achieving change by consent 139
Termination and re-employment on new terms 142
Unilateral change 144
Change pursuant to contractual rights 145

11   IDEAS FOR LOCALLY NEGOTIATED TERMS OF
    EMPLOYMENT 147
Introduction 147
Simplicity 147

CONTENTS

Incentivisation	148
Job evaluation	148
Contractual flexibility	149
Protection against competition	149
Union de-recognition	151
Index	*153*

CHAPTER 1

TERMS AND CONDITIONS OF EMPLOYMENT

INTRODUCTION – NHS TERMS OF EMPLOYMENT

For many years pay and other terms and conditions of employment have been determined centrally for the whole of the NHS by a system of Whitley Councils and Review Bodies that has evolved over the last 40 years. Each occupational group has tended to have a separate system of negotiation and consequently there has been a multiplicity of different terms and conditions. Within each set of employment terms, collective negotiation over several decades has resulted in a large number of allowances and special payments, complex rules on such things as sick leave, holiday, and acting-up.

Advantages of Whitley

1   Many of the practical questions which arise during an employee's work such as 'Can we require this employee to do this kind of work, and if so what should the employee be paid?' or 'What happens to holiday entitlement if the employee leaves part way through the year?' are covered in these terms. This certainty can be a great advantage.

2   Nationwide terms of employment have helped mobility within the NHS since staff have known what terms to expect wherever they were working. Furthermore, once employees and managers had learnt the detailed conditions of service they did not need to relearn them if they moved from one Health Service body to another.

3   The common terms of employment also recognised service with other NHS employers as continuous employment for the purpose of contractual rights such as sick pay, redundancy payments and maternity leave. This promoted mobility within the Health Service, whilst encouraging employees to remain in the public sector.

4   Although central bargaining may not have produced ideal terms and conditions for individual health service employers, it did at least relieve those employers of having to negotiate on such matters themselves. Negotiating and maintaining terms and conditions of employment with a wide range of occupational groups is a time consuming and stressful business.

Disadvantages of Whitley

1   Since the system sets out rights, obligations and allowances in detail, this has inevitably produced inflexibility. Any extra duty or task is likely to result in an entitlement to payment, and in some cases the extra duty or task cannot be required of the employee without his or her agreement. In contrast, millions of people in the UK are employed on the basis that they are paid a weekly or monthly wage or salary and have to do whatever is reasonably required of them by their employer without any right to additional remuneration.

2   Nationwide rates of pay also led to some categories of employee being overpaid (in the sense that suitably skilled people could be recruited easily at those rates of pay) and yet for other skills there might be a shortage. In practice shortages were often evaded by manipulating the common terms and conditions so as to achieve extra payments or allowances in order to attract staff. The freedom of most employers to pay whatever is required to attract the right number of the right people for that particular location is heavily circumscribed in a centralised system of this kind.

3   The detailed conditions agreed under Whitley are so complicated that in practice neither the employees to whom they apply, nor the managers who are supposed to administer them are familiar with them, let alone understand them fully.

The move away from common terms

The advent of NHS Trusts has been accompanied by a widespread move away from centrally negotiated terms. Many Trusts have negotiated local recognition agreements with the principal trade unions and have devised their own terms and conditions. The key features of the new terms are a reduction in the multiplicity of separate bargaining groups and job grades and the elimination or reduction of special allowances combined with an obligation of employees to work more flexibly. Some Trusts have also moved towards the introduction of performance related pay. Added impetus to these developments has been given by the 1995 national pay awards, where some national increases have been limited in order to give scope for local pay awards.

These developments are set out in more detail below. In most cases the new terms are offered to all new employees and to all employees accepting promotion, whilst existing staff are still employed on the centrally negotiated terms inherited by the Trusts from their predecessors. Many Trusts will have to cope with two sets of terms for some time to come. The process of change from one set of terms to another and the practical implications of the relevant law are examined in Chapter 10.

Everyone has their own ideas about what are or are not fair terms and conditions of employment. A reference in this chapter to a particular contractual term should not be taken as advising that it is either appropriate or fair – very often that question will depend upon the overall context of the employment package. What we have sought to do is to identify what the legal requirements are and, where there are options as to terms and conditions, to discuss some of the options available.

WRITTEN PARTICULARS OF EMPLOYMENT

Written particulars of employment – often called a 'Statement of Main Terms and Conditions' – have been required by law since 1963. The most recent amendment to the legal requirements was made by the Trade Union Reform and Employment Rights Act 1993 which has amended sections 1-6 of the Employment Protection (Consolidation) Act 1978. The 1993 Act required only a few additional items of information to be given, but it has significantly reduced the ability of employers to give information by cross–reference to other documents. All employers should by now have reviewed their existing Statements and brought them into line with the new legislation. If not, this needs urgent attention.

The basic legal requirements

The written particulars of employment must be issued within two months of commencement to all employees.

The statement must include the particulars set out below. The new points introduced by the 1993 Act are those shown in italics:

(a) the names of the employer and the employee;

(b) the date when the employment began;

(c) the date on which the employee's period of continuous employment began (taking into account any employment with a previous employer which counts towards that period). (Note this is not the same as 'reckonable service' under Whitley Council Conditions of Service);

(d) the scale or rate of remuneration or the method of calculating remuneration, and the intervals at which remuneration is paid;

(e) any terms or conditions relating to:

- hours of work;
- holiday entitlement (including holiday pay on termination);
- incapacity for work and sick pay;
- pension schemes;

(f) the length of notice that the employee is obliged to give and entitled to receive to terminate the contract of employment;

(g) the job title *or a brief description of the work for which the employee is employed*;

(h) *where the employment is not permanent, the period for which it is expected to continue or if it is for a fixed term the date when it is to end*;

(i) *either the place of work or an indication that the employee is required to work at various places and the address of the employer*;

(j) *particulars of any collective agreement which directly affects the terms and conditions including, where the employer is not a party, the persons by whom the collective agreement was made*;

(k) *where the person is required to work outside the UK for more than one month, the period for which the salary will be paid, any additional remuneration or benefits and any terms and conditions relating to his or her return to the UK*;

(l) a note specifying any disciplinary rules applicable to the employee or referring the employee to the provisions of a reasonably accessible document which specify such rules. The note should also include details of the person to whom the employee can apply if dissatisfied with a disciplinary decision and any person to whom he can apply for the purpose of seeking redress of any grievance.

The law does not require disciplinary *procedures* to be specified save insofar as they relate to disciplinary appeals. In practice all prudent employers cover not only disciplinary *rules* (eg forbidding theft, fighting, sexual harassment etc) and the appeal procedure, but also set out how disciplinary matters are investigated and adjudicated on prior to the appeal stage;

(m)confirmation as to whether a contracting out certificate for pension purposes is in force or not.

If there are no particulars to provide on any topic listed above, that fact must be stated.

Layout

Title – there is no legal obligation as to the title of the document. Most frequently they are referred to as 'Written Particulars of Employment' or

'Statement of Main Terms and Conditions'. Many employers also refer to the Employment Protection (Consolidation) Act 1978 in the title and even to the amending Act in 1993, but this is not required by law.

The written statement is required to contain some information which is not necessarily contractual. There are good reasons for putting this information in a separate part of the statement headed 'Information' so as to distinguish it from the remainder of the statement (which it is sensible to head 'Terms and Conditions of Employment'). There is a further discussion in relation to this topic later in this chapter.

One document, known as the 'principal statement' must contain all of the following :

(a) the names of the employer and the employee;

(b) the date when the employment began and continuous employment began;

(c) the scale or rate of remuneration and method of calculating this and the intervals at which remuneration is paid;

(d) terms and conditions relating to hours of work;

(e) terms and conditions relating to holiday entitlement and holiday pay on termination;

(f) the job title or brief job description;

(g) the place of work or indication of required or permitted places of work and the address of the employer.

All the other required matters can be in one or more other statements issued to the employee, but the items listed above must be all in a single document issued to the employee. *This is a new requirement.*

Furthermore, all of the matters required to be contained in the written particulars of employment must now be contained in the statement or statements issued to the employee, with only four exceptions. *This is a major change from the pre-1993 law* under which cross-reference to other documents was permitted without significant restriction. The only cross-references permitted in future are as follows:

(a) rules on sickness and sick pay;

(b) pension entitlement;

(c) disciplinary rules (but not disciplinary appeals or grievance procedure);

(d) the law of the land or a collective agreement in relation to notice periods.

In order for such cross-references to be permissible the document referred to must be one that the employee has reasonable opportunities of reading in the course of his employment or is made reasonably accessible to him in some other way, save that a cross-reference to the law of the land on notice rights does not need the employer to have a copy of the Act available for inspection by the employee.

These new rules on the principal statement and on cross-referencing potentially create great difficulty for health service employers who have historically issued very brief statements of main terms and conditions of employment that contained many cross-references to other documents. Indeed having to state in full holiday pay rules, acting-up rules, special allowances and the plethora of other applicable terms would be very burdensome. What are the consequences of failing to comply with this new requirement? If the employer fails to issue an adequate statement then the employee can apply to the Industrial Tribunal under section 11 of the 1978 Act for the Tribunal to specify the missing particulars. There is no fine imposed on the employer or financial award made to the employee.

In practice applications under section 11 do not usually reach the Tribunal: the employer when confronted with the application to the Tribunal will simply issue the full statement required.

It would be foolish for an employer to fail to include in the statement issued to the employee a clear indication of where the employee can find the detailed written rules on any particular point that should be covered by the written particulars. On the assumption that a clear cross-reference has been made to another document and that steps have been taken to ensure that it is readily accessible, the potential risks are low:

(a) If an employee applies to the Industrial Tribunal then, provided that clear cross-references have been made, the Tribunal will simply make a decision setting out the details. For example if the statement cross–refers to Whitley Council Conditions of Service on holiday entitlement, the Tribunal decision will set out the detailed holiday rules contained in the relevant Whitley agreement. The only potential penalty is that the Tribunal might take the view that a large employer, such as an NHS Trust, has no excuse for not providing these details in writing and therefore might order costs against the Trust. In practice, if the Trust responded to an application to the Tribunal by supplying the missing information to the individual applicant in writing and also by explaining to the Tribunal why it had decided not to issue lengthy statements setting out all the detailed terms, there must be a good prospect that a Tribunal would make a technical finding for the employee but take the matter no further.

(b) If some other issue came up before an Industrial Tribunal, such as unfair dismissal or sex discrimination, it might become apparent that an inadequate statement of the terms of employment had been issued. Provided that there was a cross-reference to a readily available document, this is unlikely to have any significant impact upon the employer's ability to defend itself in relation to the subject matter of the Tribunal hearing.

Changeover from the old rules to the new rules

There is no requirement to provide new-style statements to employees who were already working for the employer on 30 November 1993. However, any such employee can request a new-style statement and if that request is made, it must be complied with within two months (1993 Act Schedule 9 paragraph 3(3)). Such a request by the employee need not be made in writing.

Changes to terms and conditions

If there is a change to any of the terms required to be included in the statement the employee must be provided with a personal written statement detailing the changes within one month of the change (1978 Act section 4). This applies even to employees who, because they were already working for the employer in November 1993, have not been issued with a new-style statement.

It is easy to misinterpret section 4 as *entitling* an employer to change terms and conditions of employment provided that the employer gives notice of that fact within one month to employees. Nothing could be further from the truth – the Act merely requires that *if* one of the terms (whether contractual or not) required to be included in the statement of written particulars is amended – for example by agreement between the employer and employee – then this must be recorded in a written statement issued to the employee within one month of the change.

Distinction between the written particulars and the contract of employment

Every employee has a contract of employment. It may consist of written or oral express terms or of implied terms, or of any combination of the three. The legal contract between employer and employee consists of the terms upon which the employer offered employment to the employee which the employee accepted. At the extreme of informality, an oral offer 'You can start with us as a cleaner next Monday' to which the candidate responds by turning up on Monday, will be interpreted as a contract of employment on the terms and conditions then in force between the employer and other cleaners.

It is because the contract is legally binding when the offer of employment is accepted that it is prudent for employers to make sure that any special or unusual terms are brought to the employee's attention when the offer is made. For example, if you have an unusual geographical mobility clause, or a right to demote, this needs to be brought to the employee's attention when the offer is made – for example by enclosing a copy of the standard terms and conditions upon which the employee will be required to work. If this special term is not made known to the employee until later, it will not bind the employee. An offer 'on our standard terms' will be effective to incorporate the standard terms provided that you do actually have standard terms for the category of employee concerned.

As a matter of law the statement required under sections 1-4 of the Act should accurately state those contractual terms which are required, but the statement is only evidence of those terms rather than being the actual contract itself (*Parks Classic Confectionery v Ashcroft* (1973),[1] *Turriff Construction v Bland* (1967)[2] and *Robertson and Jackson v British Gas Corporation* (1983)[3]). It is open to either party to allege that the true contract is not as recorded in the written statement. More commonly one of the parties will argue that there is a term of the contract additional to those matters required by law to be included within the statement. As a matter of good practice, it is sensible for any such additional terms to be included as voluntary additional particulars in the statement given the Act.

Although the statement is not the contract, the law does say that a contract of employment in writing that contains all the information required under sections 1-4 satisfies the requirements of those sections for written particulars to be given.

As mentioned above, some of the information required in written particulars is information that need not be contractual, in particular this applies to disciplinary rules and appeal procedures and grievance procedures – section 3 of the Act requires a note of those matters to be contained in the written particulars but it does not say that they have to be part of the contract of employment. There are some persuasive reasons for ensuring that, for example, the disciplinary and grievance procedures are not contractual. First, if they are not contractual then the employer is free to change them without obtaining the individual consent of each employee. Secondly, if the employer omits a step in a disciplinary procedure that is contractual, the employee can obtain an injunction requiring the employer to follow that step through (see eg *Dietman v London Borough of Brent* (1988)[4] and *Jones v Gwent County Council* (1992)[5]). Alternatively, the employee can seek damages for the loss caused by being dismissed in breach of the procedure. These protections apply to all employees (there is no minimum qualifying period).

---

1   [1973] 8 ITR 43 DC.
2   [1967] 2 ITR 292.
3   [1983] IRLR 302 CA.
4   [1988] IRLR 299.
5   [1992] IRLR 521.

In contrast, if the disciplinary procedure is not contractual, the employee may not be able either to obtain an injunction or to obtain damages for a dismissal in breach of the disciplinary procedure and would be restricted to a claim for unfair dismissal – if the employee has adequate continuity of employment. This is an uncertain area of law and there are suggestions in the cases of *Gunton v Richmond London Borough Council* (1980),[6] *R v British Broadcasting Corporation, ex parte Lavelle* (1982)[7] and *Shook v London Borough of Ealing* (1986)[8] that even a non-contractual disciplinary procedure can be enforced by injunction and damages. Nevertheless, the freedom to change a non-contractual procedure is valuable.

Many employers include in written particulars of employment all sorts of practical everyday details such as how to apply for holidays, how uniforms should be handled, and where smoking is permitted. This temptation should be resisted – these are working rules that the employer is entitled to prescribe and to change from time to time. Indeed a prudent employer will ensure that it does revisit its rules from time to time to ensure they reflect current practice and the current needs of the organisation. These rules should therefore be separately stated – accompanied by the information that they are subject to change.

Signature to written particulars

There is no legal requirement for the employee to sign the statement. However, there are good reasons to issue two copies and to require the employee to sign and return one:

(a) this proves that the statement was issued to the employee who cannot then easily claim ignorance of its terms;

(b) doubts about which 'edition' of the statement was issued to the employee are removed;

(c) if the terms include a right to make deductions from pay under the Wages Act the formal requirements of the Act will have been met.

RIGHT TO ITEMISED PAY STATEMENT

This is another long-standing legal requirement that was amended in November 1993. All employees are entitled to an itemised pay statement (Employment Protection (Consolidation) Act 1978 section 8). The statement

---

6   [1980] ICR 755.
7   [1982] IRLR 404.
8   [1986] IRLR 46.

should set out the gross amount of the wages or salary being paid, the amounts of any deductions from that gross amount, and the net amount of wages or salary payable. Fixed deductions need not be separately stated in each wage slip if a standing statement of fixed deductions has been issued under section 9 of the Act. Such a statement must specify in relation to each deduction its amount, the intervals at which it is to be made and the purpose for which it is made. The statement of fixed deductions must be re-issued every 12 months.

CHAPTER 2

SPECIAL HEALTH SERVICE TERMS OF EMPLOYMENT

The health service has developed a number of special terms of employment. Not many of these in fact relate to the particular nature of work in the health service – they are merely the result of a long period of negotiation between unions and a public sector employer. This section looks at some of the more important employment terms which are of special relevance to the health service and also at some Whitley Council terms that are unusual.

SICK PAY

The standard Whitley Council entitlement to sick pay is shown in the following table. This is typical of the entitlement of public service employees and well in excess of that of employees in the private sector.

Period of continuous service	Period of full pay	Period of half pay
After 4 and up to 12 months	1 month	2 months
Over 1 year and up to 2 years	2 months	2 months
Over 2 years and up to 3 years	4 months	4 months
Over 3 years and up to 5 years	5 months	5 months
Over 5 years	6 months	6 months

Most groups are also entitled to one month's full pay for sickness in the first four months of service

The Conditions of Service contain arrangements to prevent the sick pay entitlements endlessly renewing themselves. On the first day of any period of absence through sickness the duration and level of entitlement for that period is identified by deducting from the employee's normal full entitlement any absences that have occurred in the previous 12 months. This means that an individual's full entitlement is only re-credited once the employee has been back at work for a full 12 months. If the employee has been back for less than 12 months then the calculation will produce a reduced sick pay figure.

In UK law, employer and employee are entirely free to agree whatever sick pay entitlement they wish, subject only to statutory sick pay being payable. Any statutory sick pay counts towards the discharge of the employer's contractual obligations to pay sick pay and any contractual payments count towards the SSP obligations.

Although the periods of sick pay typical in the NHS are generous, and it might be tempting to reduce them, it should not be forgotten that the security given by this generous sick pay is an important element in the decision of any employees to join, and stay with, the Health Service. Furthermore, it is increasingly common in the private sector for the more senior employees at least to benefit from permanent health insurance which guarantees them an income until retirement age in the event of long term disablement or sickness.

The lengthy sick pay entitlements in the Health Service can create difficulties in connection with dismissal for ill health. This is discussed later in this chapter.

Just because employees have substantial sick pay entitlement does not mean that absenteeism control should not be exercised until they have exhausted their entitlements – the patterns of absence and the reasons for absences should always be carefully monitored and steps can legally be taken to deal with the work-shy before they have exhausted their contractual entitlements.

CONTINUITY OF EMPLOYMENT

The statutory written particulars of employment must contain a statement of the date upon which the period of continuous employment began and whether employment with any previous employer counts as part of that period. Under Whitley Council terms of employment with any health service employer counts as 'reckonable service' even if there are some gaps in service. Under special regulations applying to redundancy (see below) a similar principle applies to statutory redundancy payments save that gaps in service are not bridged so readily. Statutory continuity is more restricted than each of the above.

For statutory purposes each NHS Trust, Health Authority, Health Commission etc is a separate employer and continuity is calculated on that basis (paragraphs 17(1) and 19 of Schedule 13 to the EPCA 1978 read with section 60(1) of the NHS and Community Care Act 1990).

There are only two circumstances in which statutory continuity is carried from one health service employer to another. The first relates to the calculation of redundancy payments (see below). The second is when there has been a transfer of employees together with an undertaking or a part of an undertaking governed by section 6 of the NHS and Community Care Act 1990 (creation of NHS Trusts) or by the Transfer of Undertakings (Protection of Employment) Regulations 1981 (transfers of functions such as cleaning or laundry or of clinics or departments).

The rules on continuity contained in Schedule 13 to the EPCA 1978 should be applied and the period calculated in this way stated in the written particulars. Employees may find such a statement unnerving since it may well be a shorter period than their reckonable service for Whitley Council purposes, however there is nothing to prevent the period of reckonable service also being stated.

REDUNDANCY

The General Whitley Council Conditions of Service give significant redundancy benefits to those employees to whom it applies. So far as redundancy is concerned, the calculation of service is not confined to employment with the particular employer who makes the employee redundant – under section 45 of the General Whitley Council Conditions service with any 'Health Service Authority' counts as 'Reckonable Service' for the calculation of the redundancy payment. In addition, a break in Health Service employment does not stop the earlier employment counting provided that the break did not exceed 12 months. NHS Trusts are not within the definition of 'Health Service Authority'. However, section 59 of the GWC Conditions (issued in 1990) have in effect included service in NHS Trusts as part of reckonable service for this purpose.

This is in line with amendments made with effect from 13 January 1994 to the calculation of the period of continuous employment for those employees who are entitled only to statutory redundancy payments (basically Health Service employees not employed on Whitley Council terms). That amendment was made by the Redundancy Payments (National Health Service) (Modification) Order 1993 and treats all Health Authorities and NHS Trusts as one employer for the purposes of calculating the period of continuous employment for statutory redundancy payment purposes only. It should be noted that this special calculation does not apply to any other statutory rights such as claims for unfair dismissal or entitlement to statutory maternity leave. It should also be noted that the statutory arrangement does not include a rule bridging gaps in service of up to 12 months.

In addition to dealing with the calculation of the redundancy payment, section 45 of GWC also provides that an employee loses the right to a redundancy payment if that employee unreasonably refuses an offer of suitable alternative employment with any other Health Authority or NHS Trust.

It is important to note that the questions of the suitability of the alternative employment and of whether or not it is reasonable to refuse an offer of alternative employment are not the same question. For example, a job that might normally be regarded as a suitable alternative might still be reasonably refused by an employee if it involved reporting to a supervisor with whom the employee had an unsatisfactory personal relationship. Indeed this very example was given in the case of *Milton v East Dorset Health Authority* (1990).[1]

It used to be thought that if pay is protected in the alternative post then it should be deemed suitable even if it is a lower grade post. The Employment Appeal Tribunal held in both the *Milton* case and in the case of *Knott v Southampton and South West Hampshire Health Authority* (1991)[2] that this is not so. Protection of pay merely makes the job suitable in pay terms, it may still be unsuitable if a significant demotion is involved.

The overall effect of these two decisions is that in practice the case law on what constitutes 'suitable alternative employment' and 'unreasonable refusal' in the statutory redundancy scheme is highly relevant in dealing with these two questions in the Whitley Council scheme.

The final special element of the Whitley Council redundancy scheme that should be noted is that a redundancy payment is payable in much wider circumstances that under the statutory scheme. It is payable either in a case of statutory redundancy (that is to say where the requirements of the employer for employees to carry out work of the particular kind which the employee is employed to carry out have disappeared or diminished) and also in a case of premature retirement as a result of organisational change as defined in section 46 of the GWC Conditions of Service. It is commonly assumed in the Health Service that any kind of premature retirement gives a right to a redundancy payment under section 45, but in fact early retirement in the interests of the efficiency of the service is not included in the definition of redundancy.

This makes sense in that on the one hand, an employee is entitled to a redundancy payment if the job is lost either because it has disappeared or because organisational changes mean that the employee is no longer the right person, or perhaps does not have the right skills or experience, for the job. In those circumstances the employee is losing employment because of external changes outside the employee's control. On the other hand, if early retirement is in the interests of the efficiency of the service in a situation where there is no organisational change, then the likelihood is that this is because there are deficiencies in the employee's performance or abilities, factors that are more directly attributable to the individual employee. In such a case a redundancy payment would not be appropriate.

---

1   (EAT/364/90) (unreported).

2   [1991] ICR 480.

PREMATURE RETIREMENT

The GWC Conditions of Service and the NHS Superannuation Regulations 1995 set out arrangements for the early payment of Superannuation benefits and for extra service to be credited, in four classes of premature retirement.

Premature retirement on the grounds of ill health is available to anybody suffering from permanent ill health at any age provided they have completed two years service. The service for pension calculation purposes will in the case of an employee with five or more years service be increased according to a special formula. The details are enacted in the National Health Service (Superannuation) Regulations as amended from time to time.

Premature retirement on grounds other than ill health is dealt with partly in the National Health Service (Superannuation) Regulations and partly in section 46 of the General Whitley Council conditions. The Regulations cover premature retirement on grounds of redundancy or in the interests of efficiency of the service. The intention was for amendments to be made to the Superannuation Regulations to include the right to premature retirement pension in a case of organisational change but this has never in fact occurred. It appears, therefore, that this entitlement depends upon being employed on Whitley Council terms, although it is possible that premature retirement in a case of organisational change could count as being in the interest of the efficiency of the service under the Regulations.

The uprating and the early pension are the same in all cases. In a situation where there is also an entitlement to a redundancy payment under section 45 of GWC, there are in certain circumstances abatements of the redundancy entitlements.

Two additional kinds of early retirement were introduced in March 1995. Under the first, any employee with two years service who is over the age of 50 can take an early retirement pension even if the usual conditions are not fulfilled. This is conditional on the employer agreeing to meet the extra pension costs. The second new arrangement does not require the consent of the employer, or any contribution by the employer. However, the pension will be automatically reduced.

These provisions enabling premature retirement are very useful management tools in the NHS. A premature retirement is not cost free for the employing body since it has to make a contribution to the retirement benefits, but nevertheless there are in practice many possibilities for achieving a severance for a long term employee with much less pain than if these provisions did not exist. Indeed, in many cases the premature retirement regime is sufficiently generous that the employee will welcome the termination. This is discussed further in Chapter 7.

PROTECTION OF EARNINGS

Section 47 of the GWC Conditions of Service provides for the protection of the earnings of any employee who is required by management to move to a new post as a consequence of organisational change. It also applies to an employee who suffers a reduction in basic hours for the same reason. Section 47 expires on 30 September 1995. Employees under protection on that date will retain their rights. Whitley Council has recommended that in future protection should be a topic for local agreement. No doubt the old scheme will serve as a model for many local agreements.

Under the Whitley Council scheme there there are three protections: short term protection of earnings whether or not downgrading is involved, long term protection of basic wage or salary where downgrading is involved and protection of certain other conditions for service.

By 'downgrading' section 47 means being moved to a new post carrying a lower hourly rate or carrying a salary scale with a maximum point lower than that applying to the post held previously.

Even if downgrading is not involved, an employee can suffer if the overtime and special allowances are lower in the new post. Accordingly, employees are entitled to a limited period of protection even if downgrading is not involved, ranging from two months protection for those with between four and 12 months service and 12 months protection for those with five years service or more. During that period the employee is entitled to his or her average earnings in the four months immediately preceding the change of job. If in any particular pay period the earnings in the new job exceed those in the old job then clearly the protection does not apply for that period.

In a case where downgrading is involved, then the protection is much longer in its duration. The protection is of basic wage or salary only but the employee is entitled during the protection period to the benefit of any increases in the basic wage or salary of the old job. For most employees the period of protection is one year for each year of service up to a maximum of five years. However, long service employees over the age of 41 can get longer periods of protection, up to a maximum of 15 years. Even once the period of protection has come to an end, the employee's pay is not actually reduced but the pay is frozen on a mark time basis until the pay in the new job catches up.

Because the long term protection is indeed so long in its duration, there are elaborate provisions relating to changes in job that can limit the period of protection. An employee moving from one employer operating Whitley to another can carry the protection with him or her which means that recruiting employers should be careful to try to identify in advance whether this protection applies.

The third element of protection is other terms and conditions of service such as subsistence and travel, notice periods, annual leave and so on. Some of those protections apply only to those who are in receipt of long term downgrading protection.

It is all too easy to assume that because a contractual arrangement for the protection of pay exists and because of the reference in the opening paragraph of section 47 to an employee being 'required by management' to move to a new post, that an employee can indeed be compelled to change jobs in a situation of organisational change. This is not the case. Section 47 merely spells out the contractual entitlements of the employee if he or she agrees to the move but, unless something has been spelt out specifically in the contract of employment of that particular employee, he or she cannot be required to move.

Of course, if an employee does decline to move then the employer may decide to terminate the employment. Such a termination will, on the face of things, entitle the employee to a redundancy payment under section 45 of the GWC Conditions of Service. However, section 45 makes it absolutely clear that the redundancy payment is not available if the employee unreasonably refuses suitable alternative employment. The cases of *Milton v East Dorset Health Authority* (1990)[3] and *Knott v Southampton and South West Hampshire Health Authority* (1991)[4] were about this very topic. The employment appeals tribunal held in both cases that the mere fact that protection of earnings would apply did not make a job suitable in all respects – questions of demotion, having to work for unsuitable bosses and so on were still relevant (see further *supra*).

The very existence of protection of pay can significantly reduce the value to employers of reorganisations that were intended to increase efficiency or create savings by producing a better match of employees to the work that is required to be done. There is something to be said for contracts of employment that do not carry this protection within them so that each case be approached on an *ad hoc* basis on its individual merits.

CONFIDENTIALITY AND RELATIONS WITH THE PUBLIC MEDIA

Introduction

Until recently it has not been normal for Health Service employers to include express terms on confidentiality in contracts of employment. That does not mean that employees do not owe a duty of confidentiality to their employer and indeed it is well established that such duties do exist by implication.

There are two main categories of confidential information that employees in the Health Service become party to. One is information relating to the medical condition and history of patients. The other is information relating to the affairs of their employer.

---

[3] (EAT/364/90) (unreported).

[4] [1991] ICR 480.

Patient information

Of course, many Health Service workers have professional obligations in relation to patient information and can be disciplined by their professional bodies for not respecting those obligations. However, all the Health Service employees have, in addition, implied obligations under their contracts of employment to respect the confidentiality of such information.

In August 1994 the Department of Health published a consultation paper on draft guidance intending to clarify the law and procedures in relation to patient confidential information.

The obligation with regard to information concerning patients is not an absolute one and in particular it is subject to the following exceptions or conditions:

1 information can be disclosed if the patient has expressly consented;

2 information can be disclosed to others involved in treating the patient – even here, some information may be particularly personal or embarrassing and care should be taken to avoid information becoming more widespread, even within the Health Service, than is necessary;

3 information may be ordered to be disclosed by court order. If in doubt when asked to disclose information it is prudent for the possessors of it, having taken advice from their professional bodies or defence organisations and from their employers, to consider in many cases putting the issue to the courts so as to enable the courts to reach a conclusion;

4 on occasions the disclosure of confidential information is required by statute, such as under various Public Health Regulations and the Health and Safety at Work Act;

5 finally, disclosure can be made in the public interest. The categories of public interest are not, in law, closed. Some categories are well established and others can be assumed to exist although in fact it has not been conclusively demonstrated in the Courts that they do.

It is established that public interest includes protecting others from serious risk whether to health or otherwise. For example, the courts have sanctioned local authorities disclosing information that they held confidentially about children subject to their care in order to protect other children who might be at risk (*Re F* (1989),[5] *Re M* (1990)[6] and *Re A* (1992)[7]). Such disclosure is of course only protected in so far as it is made to the right people and is no more extensive than is necessary.

---

5   [1989] 1 FLR 39.
6   [1990] 2 FLR 36.
7   [1992] 1 All ER 153.

Again, disclosure for the prevention, detection or prosecution of serious crime is a well established exception in law.

It is believed that disclosure as part of bona fide approved clinical and scientific research and surveys and for the reporting of adverse drug reactions is justified, on the basis that it is in the overall public interest that such information should be disclosed, but there is no clear legal authority to confirm this.

The final category where public interest is typically relied upon is in relation to public accountability and monitoring purposes, such as for the collection of statistics. In such cases, particular care should be given to ensure that the identifiable details, before they become mere statistics, are not disseminated further than is reasonable and stay within the employer's organisation, or at least within the Health Service as a whole.

The affairs of the employer

The second main category of confidential information that comes within the knowledge of Health Service employees is information relating to the affairs and management of their particular employer. This has of course been an area of great controversy in recent years and a number of NHS Trusts have introduced express clauses in terms and conditions of employment requiring confidentiality to be observed.

The NHS Management Executive in June 1993 published guidance on this topic under the title 'Guidance for staff on relations with the public and the media'. This guidance makes the point that even when there is no express confidentiality clause in the contract of employment, all employees have an implied duty of confidentiality and loyalty to their employer. What is not clear, particularly in a Health Service context, is how far that duty goes. In the new internal market NHS it probably goes a lot further than it did only a few years ago since the clear public policy, as demonstrated by the NHS and Community Care Act 1990, is that there should be competition amongst Trusts as providers and bargaining between providers and purchasers. In those circumstances information that at one time could have been passed between different parts of the Health Service without any concern at all clearly becomes confidential information.

On the other hand, employees may become aware of information that could be published without significant risk of damaging the employer from the competitive point of view but that nevertheless the management of the Trust would prefer not to make public because, for example, it would expose inefficiency or mismanagement within the Trust. This area has not yet been legally tested but there is a likelihood that disclosure of such information by an employee would be a breach of the implied duty of loyalty, even if there was no express clause.

Having said that, the public interest again intervenes in this field of confidentiality and it is clear that no court would consider an employee to have been in breach of his or her contract of employment if they had made public some matter of serious public concern about the National Health Service (which is after all a public service). To be confident of protection by the courts the employee would want to make sure that he or she had done everything possible to resolve the issue without publicity. These are the very principles outlined in the guidance issued by the NHSME, which urges Health Service employers to establish clear procedures through which employees can raise matters of concern about the organisation and management of their employer. The purpose of those formal procedures, apart from ensuring that matters of concern do come to the attention of those responsible, is to give the employer material that it can use to demonstrate to a court that the employee has breached or is proposing to breach, unnecessarily and unreasonably, his or her duty of confidence. Health Service employers should therefore ensure that they do have a formal procedure in place and that it is well publicised. Given that guidance has been given to Health Service employers that they should have such procedures, an employer who does not have a procedure is going to be in a weak position in court if it seeks to argue that an employee has too readily gone public.

As mentioned above, this whole area has become much more significant since the development of the internal market and we can expect in coming years some cases to reach the courts that will confirm, or undermine, the application of these general principles, which are derived from employment in the private sector, to the Health Service situation.

CHAPTER 3

MATERNITY RIGHTS

HISTORICAL BACKGROUND

Until October 1994 most employees in the UK had only the benefit of statutory maternity leave which depended upon two years continuous service with their current employer and upon complying with the statutory notification requirements. In contrast, the General Whitley Council maternity arrangements were considerably more generous. The main entitlement to maternity leave under section 6 of the GWC Conditions of Service was up to one year's leave provided that the employee has one year's 'continuous service' with any Health Service employer. For those employees who did not qualify for the main right, there was a reduced entitlement of 18 weeks maternity leave for all full-time employees and for those part-time employees who were entitled to normal sick pay when absent through sickness.

Where an employee is entitled to both statutory and contractual maternity rights, the law provides that the employee can pick and choose the best of each right. In the Health Service this nearly always meant relying upon Whitley Council and consequently the old statutory maternity right had very little influence.

A similar situation pertained in relation to maternity pay for any employee with at least a year's continuous service, since she would be entitled under Whitley Council conditions to full pay for the first eight weeks of her maternity leave followed by 10 weeks at half pay – a provision that is considerably more generous than statutory maternity pay.

The implementation in the UK in October 1994 of the European Pregnant Workers Directive has significantly changed the position. Whilst the old statutory maternity rights remain for those with two years' continuous employment, there is a new right for all employees, no matter how short their service and how few their hours of work per week, to 14 weeks of maternity leave. Any reference to 'maternity leave' or 'the maternity leave period' in statutory materials is now a reference to this new 14 week right and the old statutory maternity leave is referred to as 'the right to return'. In practice, most people are referring the old right as 'extended maternity leave'.

The new statutory maternity leave had an impact on maternity arrangements under Whitley Council Conditions since for some categories of employees the new statutory right was better than their contractual rights. Primarily this affected NHS employees with less than one year's continuous service for Whitley Council maternity leave purposes. In addition, the statutory rules as to how maternity rights are exercised apply not only to statutory maternity leave but also to contractual maternity leave. In consequence the amendments made with effect from October 1994 to the statutory procedural requirements also have an automatic impact on the procedural rules for both kinds of Whitley Council maternity leave.

An NHS employer who did nothing therefore faced the following situation:

- three maternity leave rights (statutory maternity leave, 18 weeks maternity leave and one year's maternity leave);

- alterations to procedural requirements for exercising maternity rights.

- employees entitled to 18 weeks or one year's maternity leave under Whitley Council relying upon the new 14 week statutory right to improve some aspects of their maternity leave entitlement.

Not surprisingly, most NHS employers examined simplification, as did Whitley Council. Whitley Council has adopted the simplest solution which is to harmonise the 18 week maternity leave entitlement of Whitley Council Conditions with the statutory 14 week right and to make some minor amendments to the rules for one year's maternity leave. This approach has obviously resulted in some increase in cost.

THE DETAIL

Statutory maternity leave

The legal provisions which set out this right are contained in the new sections 33-38A of the Employment Protection (Consolidation) Act 1978 which were introduced by the 1993 Act. Any employee, irrespective of her length of service and hours of work, is entitled to 14 weeks' statutory maternity leave. She is entitled to choose to start her leave on any date from the beginning of the 11th week before the expected week of childbirth.

The employee must give 21 days notice to the employer of:

- the fact that she is pregnant;

- the expected week of confinement; and

- the fact that she intends to exercise her right to take maternity leave.

If adequate notice cannot be given it must be given as soon as reasonably practicable. The employer is entitled to ask for medical evidence (usually produced in the form MAT B1) of the pregnancy although no date for production of this evidence is prescribed by law.

The employee does not need to give notice that she intends to return. Furthermore, she is not required to give notice to the employer prior to coming back to work – she just needs to present herself at the end of the 14th week. If she wishes to return to work early she must give the employer at least seven days notice.

During the period of maternity leave the employee is entitled to all the benefits and terms and conditions of being an employee save 'remuneration'. The meaning of this word has not been defined in the legislation and awaits interpretation in the case law. It clearly means that the employee has no entitlement to pay but that an employee does continue to accrue, for example, holiday entitlement. In the 'grey area' are cash allowances (such as essential car-user allowances and uniform allowances) and pension scheme membership. Most lawyers (including the authors) are of the view that pension scheme membership must continue, but that allowances are more debatable. In the case of allowances the answer may be affected by whether or not some employees receive the benefit in kind rather than in cash – if they do then it is more likely that the allowances will not be seen as remuneration.

All employees are protected against dismissal for taking advantage of their statutory and contractual maternity leave rights – they can claim unfair dismissal without any minimum service qualification.

Whitley Council maternity rights

The main entitlement under the GWC Conditions of Service is to one year's maternity leave commencing on or after the beginning of the 11th week before the expected week of child birth. This right brings with it an entitlement to pay for the first eight weeks of leave at full rate and at half rate for the following 10 weeks. This right applies to any woman with at least 12 months of 'continuous service', which includes employment by any NHS employer. Gaps of up to three months (and in some cases longer gaps) will be disregarded in determining whether or not the service is continuous. Apart from these special rules, 'continuous service' is defined in the same way as a 'period of employment' in Schedule 13 of the Employment Protection (Consolidation) Act 1978. This meant that certain part-timers were excluded. The Act has been amended with effect from 6 February 1995, so as to include all part-timers. In the authors' view this also amends the Whitley Council definition, with the consequence that all part-timers and full-timers qualify for one year's maternity leave after one year's service.

Employees without adequate continuous employment are entitled, if they are full or part-timers who are entitled to sick pay, to maternity leave without pay for up to 18 weeks.

The notification rules for both kinds of Whitley Council maternity leave are the same. The employee is required at least 21 days before the absence commences to give notice of:

- the fact that she is pregnant;
- the expected week of childbirth;
- the fact that she intends to take leave; and
- that she intends to return to work.

If adequate notice cannot be given it must be given as soon as reasonably practicable. She is also required to submit confirmation from a doctor or midwife that she is pregnant and the expected date of child birth.

The woman used to be required to start her maternity leave in the 11th week before the EWC unless she provided medical evidence that she was fit to continue to work. This condition is no longer lawful and section 6 of the GWC now makes it clear that a woman can choose any date to start her leave from the beginning of the 11th week before the expected week of childbirth to the expected date of childbirth. However maternity leave is triggered if a woman is absent from work through pregnancy related illness at any time after the beginning of the sixth week before the expected week of childbirth. If an employee is sick after she has started her maternity leave she is not entitled to sick pay – she is on maternity leave.

If the woman is suspended from work with pay during pregnancy because of a health risk, when does her maternity leave period start – can she postpone it to the very last minute in order to maximise her income? Statutory maternity leave is triggered by absence from work during or after the sixth week before the EWC, wholly or partly for any reason connected with pregnancy. There is therefore a strong argument that statutory maternity leave for such a woman starts automatically at the beginning of the sixth week before the EWC. The position is not so clear under the GWC, but the strong implication of paragraph 7 of section 6 is that the same rule applies.

When the woman intends to return she has to give 21 days written notice of her intention to return.

Not earlier than 49 days after the expected week of childbirth (or 11 weeks after the start of maternity leave, whichever is the later), the employer can write to the employee asking for confirmation that she does intend to exercise her right to return. Note the words in brackets in the previous sentence that represent an amendment to the Whitley rules that reflect the new statutory rules. The employee must be warned that failure to respond positively will result in her losing her right to return.

A woman who does not intend to return to work after the baby's birth but has two years service is entitled to six weeks maternity leave with pay at nine-tenths of full pay, followed by eight weeks of SMP.

A woman who gives notice of her intention to return to work, but does not in fact do so with her former employer or with another Health Service employer within 15 months of the beginning of her maternity leave, is obliged to refund the whole of her maternity pay received, less any statutory maternity pay to which she was entitled.

Under new paragraph 28 of section 6, a woman is now entitled to the benefit of all terms and conditions of employment, other than remuneration and accrual of holiday, for the whole of her maternity leave period. This is considerably more generous than the statutory scheme and could obviously be expensive since it will include all benefits in kind. For example, an employee who is entitled to use a car supplied by her employer for private purposes will retain that right during her maternity leave period. For the rules on holiday accrual see paragraph 2 of the 'Traps' section below.

Compulsory maternity leave

By virtue of the Maternity (Compulsory Leave) Regulations 1994, if a woman has complied with the notice requirements for basic statutory maternity leave she must not be permitted to work for two weeks after the day of childbirth. 'Day of Childbirth' is defined to mean the birth of a living child or a still birth occurring after 24 weeks of pregnancy.

Traps arising from discrepancies between statutory 14 week maternity leave and the Whitley Council rights

1   A woman is entitled to return after 14 weeks even if she did not give notice of intention to return – it is enough that her notice stated, 'I intend to take maternity leave'. Arguably, under the 'best of both worlds rule' this would apply also to return after 18 weeks, but the authors think not.

2   A woman taking the 14 week right can come back to work at the end of the 14 weeks without giving any advance notice, and if she comes back earlier she need give only seven days notice. Section 6 of GWC could mislead in this respect since it refers to 21 days notice of intended date of return. The 21 day notice applies to the contractual right to up to one year's maternity leave. It is not clear whether under the 'best of both worlds rule' the employee can avoid giving 21 days notice if she is relying on the 18 week maternity leave right under GWC. The author's view is that there is a strong argument that the employee taking 18 weeks must give 21 days notice.

3   Under new paragraph 30 of section 6, holiday entitlement only accrues during the paid part of maternity leave, in most cases 18 weeks. However, employees with less that one year's service are not entitled to 'paid maternity leave' within the meaning of this term in section 6. Such

employees will be entitled to SMP if they have six months service and to maternity allowance from the state if they have less than six months service. One might read paragraph 30 to mean that they had no entitlement to accrue holiday during any part of their maternity leave, however, both categories will be entitled to accrue holiday for the 14 weeks of the statutory maternity leave.

Publish a maternity policy

Once an employer has decided how it is going to deal with maternity rights it is vital that it should publish a maternity policy. Employees will inevitably be confused because maternity rights are so complicated and because of the difficult inter-relationship of traditional NHS maternity leave rights and the statutory minima. A coherent practical guide to the rights is vital to ensure that consistent rules are applied to all female employees and to ensure that the law is obeyed.

A maternity policy can also deal with topics like time off for ante-natal care, return to work part-time and job sharing.

What job is the employee entitled to return to?

Slightly different wording has been used in, on the one hand, the provisions introducing the new statutory right to 14 weeks leave and, on the other hand, the old statutory right to return and Whitley Council maternity leave. In relation to the latter, the employee is entitled to return to her 'job', and the case law decisions indicate that this is to be determined by reference to both the employee's contract and, to some extent at least, the actual work she was doing. Until recently there were good grounds to think, following cases on the law of redundancy, that if the range of work which the employee could be required to carry out under a contract was wide, then her 'job' would be wide for this purpose also. The recent decision of *Bass Leisure Ltd v Thomas* (1994)[1] suggests that a 'job' may now have a narrower meaning.

In contrast, in respect of the 14 week maternity leave right, the right is expressly for the employee to return under her contract and this must make it possible to move her to any other work within her contract – although to do so without good reason would expose the employer to possible claims for constructive dismissal or even sex discrimination, on the basis that the adverse treatment was a penalty imposed on the woman for exercising her maternity rights. Further, since section 6 of GWC applies the 'job' wording to both the full one year leave and the shorter 18 week leave, it would be unwise for an employer to try to rely on this argument about the 14 week statutory right.

---

[1]   [1994] IRLR 104.

What if it is not practicable for the employer to take the employee back?

There are three possibilities:

(a) It is not practicable to take the employee back because of redundancy. In such circumstances any 'suitable available vacancy' must be offered to the employee. The contract of employment for the vacancy must be such that the work to be done under the contract is of a kind which is both suitable in relation to the employee and appropriate for her to do in the circumstances. The provisions of the new contract as to capacity and place in which she is to be employed and as to other terms and conditions, must be not substantially less favourable than if she was still doing her old job. Although the Act does not say this, 'suitable' clearly implies that vacancies only have to be offered to employees if they are capable of performing them.

If a suitable available vacancy exists but is not offered to the employee then she is automatically unfairly dismissed irrespective of her length of service. This is important in the Health Service where it often occurs that a number of employees are potentially redundant and they are asked to compete for alternative employment. If an employee on maternity leave was required to compete rather than be placed in the job, she would have an undefeatable claim for unfair dismissal.

(b) It is not reasonably practicable for the employer to take the employee back for reasons other than redundancy, but an alternative post is available. The failure to take the employee back will be a deemed dismissal giving her a potential right to claim unfair dismissal. However, there is no deemed dismissal if the employer has offered suitable alternative employment to the employee and she has unreasonably turned it down (section 56A EPCA). Again, the offer must be of work which is suitable in relation to the employee and appropriate for her to do in the circumstances and the terms and conditions must not be substantially less favourable.

(c) It is not reasonably practicable for the employer to let the employee return but there is no suitable alternative work available. In these circumstances there is a deemed dismissal (section 56 EPCA 1978) and the employer will have to establish that the dismissal was fair by reference to one of the usual potentially fair grounds for dismissal. Section 57 of the Act, which sets out the basis upon which the Tribunal should assess fairness is amended for this purpose by paragraph 2(1) of Schedule 2 to the Act so that the question about fairness must be asked on the assumption that the employee had not been away from work.

Rights after return to work

On return the employee is entitled to the pay and benefits to which she would have been entitled had she not been away. For the purposes of calculation of seniority, the 14 week period counts. Any further absence, whether under statutory or contractual maternity leave, does not count, but it also does not break seniority – in other words the service prior to the leave and the service after the leave are joined together for this purpose. It should be noted that statutory continuity of employment continues to accrue during maternity leave.

Enforcement of maternity rights and protection against dismissal

If an employer breaks an employee's maternity rights then the employee's remedy is through a claim for unfair dismissal. In some circumstances a failure to permit a woman to return to work is classified as a special 'deemed dismissal' by section 56 of the Employment Protection (Consolidation) Act 1978. Even where deemed dismissal does not apply, the contract of employment will usually have remained in force during the period of maternity leave (*Hilton International Hotels Limited v Kaissi* (1994)[2]) and therefore an ordinary claim for unfair dismissal may be possible. In addition, a claim of unlawful discrimination under the Sex Discrimination Act, as interpreted by the European Court, is quite likely.

This section outlines the legal position and then tries to examine how the protections apply in practice. The law in this area is not particularly clear and the views set out below are a combination of the authors' opinions on the correct interpretation of the relevant statutes, together with their prediction as to likely case law decisions. There is bound to be continuing case law development in this field over the coming years and therefore the up-to-date state of the legal authorities should always be checked.

Dismissal on grounds of pregnancy or child birth

Any dismissal for one of these reasons or for a reason connected with one of these reasons is automatically unfair irrespective of the employee's length of service.

Dismissal for taking advantage of maternity leave rights

Any such dismissal is automatically unfair irrespective of the employee's length of service.

---

2   [1994] IRLR 270.

Employee who fails to follow the statutory or contractual rules applying to her maternity leave

This is an area where the law is both confused and uncertain. For some time the Court of Appeal and Employment Appeal Tribunal Judges have been complaining about the confusion and indeed they have delivered judgments on this question of dismissal and maternity leave in which they have said that they are not sure that they have correctly interpreted the statute! That difficulty has been compounded by recent European Court decisions on the law of sex discrimination and by the additional complications introduced by the new right to basic maternity leave for 14 weeks. All that can really be said at the moment is that there are three legal possibilities:

1   That if an employee fails in any respect to comply with her obligations, for example, by giving a defective notice of some kind or by failing to return to work on the correct date, then she has lost all her rights. There are cases which support this view (*Addlestone v McKnight*[3] (1984) and *Lavery v Plessey Communications* (1981),[4] which were decisions of the Northern Ireland Court of Appeal and the English Court of Appeal respectively). However, the most recent authority, in the more junior Employment Appeal Tribunal, in the case of *Kaissi v Hilton International Hotels* (1994)[5] undermines this.

2   That in most circumstances the contract of employment persists through maternity leave and that an employee can therefore claim unfair dismissal even if she has failed to comply with statutory rules.

    This is largely the approach taken by the Employment Appeal Tribunal in the *Kaissi* case but it does create difficulties. For example, if the employee has failed by one day to give adequate notice of her intention to take maternity leave or of her intended date of return, she would appear to fall outside the statutory rights and yet it would be very difficult for an employer to say that it was fair and reasonable to dismiss her for that very small failing. On the other hand, if it is not fair for an employer to dismiss in those circumstances, the very basis of the strict statutory time limits is undermined. At the very least therefore, one would expect Tribunals to give considerable weight, in assessing fairness or unfairness, to the fact that the employee had failed to fulfil the statutory requirements.

3   That some kind of mixture between 1 and 2 above applies. The most likely mixture would be that once an employee has sought to exercise her right to return towards the end of her maternity leave, then if she fails to comply with the legal requirements at that point she will have no right to complain. (It is clear that this is the law if the employee is seeking to

---

3   [1984] IRLR 453.
4   [1981] IRLR 202 CA.
5   [1994] IRLR 270.

exercise a contractual right to return – *Lavery v Plessey Telecommunications* applying paragraph 6(2) of Schedule 2 to the EPCA.) On the other hand, if her error has been made at an earlier stage, any dismissal by the employer will have to be judged on the ordinary basis as to whether or not it is fair.

This line of argument helps to reconcile the decided cases but has little inherent logic to recommend it – why should the 21 day time limit for notices matter more in relation to the notice of the intended date of return than in relation to the notice of the intention to take maternity leave in the first place?

In view of the confused legal situation, what practical steps can be taken by an employer faced with an employee who has not entirely complied with the statutory and contractual maternity rules? The practical advice is:

- if the employee's failure relates to what she has done when seeking to return after contractual maternity leave (eg under the Whitley Council scheme) then she need not be allowed to return and there is no dismissal of which she can complain;

- in all other cases, investigate the circumstances of the case and if necessary give the employee a hearing about them. If the employee's failure is minor or if the employee has not been irrevocably replaced, it would be prudent to let the employee return. Even if after investigation the decision is made not to let her return, there is at least a chance of establishing fair dismissal on the basis that there has been a full enquiry into the situation and the employer's managers have applied their minds to the situation rather than operated automatic rules.

So far in this section we have only mentioned unfair dismissal, but there is also a role for the law of sex discrimination. If an employee who is outside her statutory or contractual maternity leave rights can show that a man in similar circumstances would have been treated more favourably, she may well have a good claim for sex discrimination. She might, for example, want to draw a parallel with a man who had been absent from work through ill health for a period of time.

Until 1994, it was clear that this would have been a good line of argument for a woman under United Kingdom sex discrimination law. However, in the European Court of Justice case *Webb v EMO Cargo UK Ltd* (1994)[6] the European Court of Justice held that in order to establish sex discrimination a woman who was pregnant or had recently given birth did not have to compare herself with a man who had had a period of absence for a similar purpose (such as an operation). The Court said that maternity cannot be compared with a pathological condition.

---

[6]   C-32/93 [1994] IRLR 482 ECJ.

It is not clear whether the ban on such a comparison applies only where making such a comparison imposes an extra hurdle for a woman to overcome in claiming sex discrimination, or whether it also debars her from relying upon that comparison to establish sex discrimination. This issue may well be settled by the *Gillespie* case. The course of prudence in an uncertain state of law is to consider the position of 'comparable' men before making a final decision about a woman in relation to maternity leave.

Pay during maternity and the law of sex discrimination

This is another area where the law of sex discrimination may have an effect on maternity rights. If a woman taking maternity leave can compare her treatment to that afforded by the employer to a man then it must be open to a woman employed, for example, on Whitley Council terms to claim up to six months full pay and six months half pay, plus benefits such as a lease car, during her absence on maternity leave on the basis that if she were a man away on sick leave, she would have that entitlement. This issue has been referred by the Court of Appeal in Northern Ireland to the European Court of Justice in the case of *Gillespie*. The argument is strengthened by reference to the Pregnant Workers Directive, which itself states in Article 11(3) that maternity pay should be at least equivalent to sick pay. This has been interpreted by the UK government as a reference to comparison with Statutory Sick Pay, but this is not clear.

Obviously the expense to Trusts if this argument were to succeed would be very substantial. Until the issue has been settled by the courts, the authors would expect health service employers not to make payments beyond the contractual maternity obligations.

Maternity rights and fixed term contracts

Women are entitled to maternity leave and maternity pay under both the statutory and Whitley Council schemes, even if they are employed on fixed term contracts. If a fixed term contract expires during the period of maternity leave then the situation is different from that of employees on ordinary indefinite contracts. Once again there are some doubts about the legal technicalities in such a situation.

So far as the Whitley Council scheme is concerned, if the woman was in a training rotation of a fixed duration then the rotation is 'frozen' until the end of her maternity leave and then restarted on her return. The Whitley Council conditions also extend all fixed terms so as to enable the employee to receive her full entitlement to maternity pay.

Apart from those two special rules, the ordinary statutory Whitley Council schemes apply. For most, if not all, purposes in relation to maternity leave, the non-renewal of a fixed term contract will amount to a 'dismissal' giving the employee the ability to try to establish that the dismissal was unfair. If the employer's need for her work has come to an end then it is likely that the dismissal will be readily accepted as fair. On the other hand, if the likelihood is that the employment would have been renewed had she been at work, it is likely that the failure to renew it will be an unfair dismissal. In other words, the employer should be able to defend the non-renewal on the same basis as he would defend it had the employee not been absent at the time the contract expired.

Of course if the fixed term contract is for at least one year and the employee has signed a contract containing the appropriate contracting out wording, then she will not be able to bring any claim in respect of the non-renewal even if it occurred in connection with pregnancy or maternity.

Suspension on health and safety grounds

Until the recent reform of statutory maternity rights, it was lawful to dismiss a woman who could not carry out her work for health and safety reasons associated with pregnancy or maternity. This is no longer the case. Instead, such women are entitled to alternative employment and failing that to be suspended on full pay.

New sections 45-47 of the Employment Protection (Consolidation) Act 1978 apply when a woman is suspended from work on the grounds that she is pregnant, has recently given birth or is breast feeding because of any requirement imposed by or under any statutory provision or in accordance with any recommendation in a Code of Practice issued under the Health & Safety at Work Act.

There are a number of statutory provisions preventing employment of mothers and mothers-to-be which are set out in the table below. In addition, under Regulation 13A of the Management of Health and Safety at Work Regulations 1992, the risk assessment that every employer must make as to health and safety risks for employees must include the risks for pregnant women, women who have recently given birth and those who are breast feeding. Under those Regulations, if a risk is identified steps must be taken to avoid it, by altering her conditions or hours of work. If such an alteration is unreasonable or would not avoid the risk then alternative employment, and failing that suspension, will be required.

All employers should obtain a copy of the *Health & Safety Executive Guide for Employers 'New and Expectant Mothers at Work'*,[7] which gives useful

---

7   ISBN 0-7176-0826-3.

practical guidance. The guidance is not however entirely accurate in that it suggests at some points in the text that action must be taken only if the woman would be exposed to 'significant' risk, whereas no such word is used in the Regulations. According to the Regulations, if there would be any risk to the health of the mother or the baby then it must be avoided. The only qualification on this is in relation to infectious or contagious disease where the Regulations specify that such a risk only counts for action if the level of risk at work is additional to the level at which the mother might be expected to be exposed outside the work place. It would seem therefore, that exposure to, for example, the common cold which is probably no more likely at work than at home, would not lead to action being necessary whereas exposure from working on a hospital ward in which there are people suffering from infectious diseases would require such action.

There are also special rules relating to night workers. Under Regulation 13B of the Management of Health & Safety at Work Regulations 1992, where a new or expectant mother (ie an employee who is pregnant or who has given birth within the previous six months or is breast feeding) works at night she may be provided with a certificate from a doctor or midwife about night working. If she has a certificate which shows that it is 'necessary for her health or safety' that she should not be at work for any night hours specified in the certificate then the employer must either offer her alternative employment or, failing that, suspend her for so long as is necessary for her health or safety.

There is no definition of 'night work' in the Regulations or in the European Directive from which they are derived. Ultimately the European Court of Justice may make a decision about this but in the meantime employers will just have to take a sensible approach. In practice therefore, any hours forbidden by a doctor or midwife in a certificate should be accepted unless they are plainly hours that everyone would call daytime hours.

It should be noted that the certificate should only be given if the fact that the work is at night causes the health and safety risk – if the employer considers that the practitioner merely feels that the woman should not be working at all, then the position could be tested by asking the practitioner to explain why it is that night work is inappropriate. Of course the practitioner might refuse to answer, in which case the practical course of action for the employer is to test the situation by finding daytime work for the employee and seeing what happens.

Intriguingly, the HSE Guidance is that they are not aware of any risks to pregnant or breast feeding workers or their children which arise from working at night. On that basis one might think that a doctor's or midwife's certificate could be challenged, but there is no mechanism in the legislation to do so. It would seem that the certificate must be accepted at face value unless it is an obvious sham.

Summary of hazards, risks and ways of avoiding them

(The following table is a summary of the detailed guidance table contained in the HSE document 'New and Expectant Mothers at Work – a Guide for Employers'):

Activity or agent	Risks arising	Relevant rules
Shocks, vibration or movement	Risks during pregnancy and shortly after giving birth	
Manual handling of loads	Risks during pregnancy and for people who have recently given birth in certain circumstances	Manual Handling Operations Regulations 1992
Noise	Prolonged exposure to loud noise may lead to increased blood pressure and tiredness	Noise at Work Regulations 1989
Ionising Radiation	Risks to the foetus and nursing mother	Ionising Radiation Regulations 1985 and supporting Code of Practice
Non-ionising electro-magnetic radiation	No special risks from optical radiation Extreme over exposure to radio frequency radiation could cause harm by raising body temperature	
Extremes of cold or heat	Risks for women when pregnant or breast feeding or have recently given birth	
Movements and postures, travelling, mental and physical fatigue and physical burdens	Risks for pregnant women and women who have recently given birth	
Working in hyperbaric atmosphere	Risk for those who are pregnant or have recently given birth	Work in Compressed Air Special Regulations 1958 and the Diving Operations at Work Regulations 1981
Biological agents of hazards groups 2, 3 & 4	Risks for women who are pregnant or breast feeding or have recently given birth	Control of Substances Hazardous to Health Regulations 1994 and approved Code of Practice on the control of biological agents

Activity or agent	Risks arising	Relevant rules
Substances labelled R40, R45, R46, R47 (soon to be R61, R62 and R64) under Directive 67/548/EEC	Risks to unborn children and breast fed babies	Control of Substances Hazardous to Health Regulations 1994 and Hazardous Chemicals Information and Packaging Regulations 1993
Other chemical agents and industrial processes		Control of Substances Hazardous to Health Regulations 1994
Mercury and mercury derivatives	Risks during pregnancy	
Antimitotic (Cytotoxic) Drugs	Risks to fertility	Control of Substances Hazardous to Health Regulations 1994
Chemical agents of known and dangerous percutaneous absorption	Risks not specified in the guidance	Control of Substances Hazardous to Health Regulations 1994 and Control of Pesticides Regulations 1986
Carbon monoxide	Risks during pregnancy	
Lead and lead derivatives	Risks during pregnancy and breast feeding	Control of Lead at Work Regulations 1980 and associated Code of Practice
Work with display screen equipment (VDUs)	No evidence of special risk	

Before suspending a women because of a risk to her health or safety the employer must, under section 46, consider whether he can offer suitable alternative employment. This involves taking into account whether or not the work is suitable in relation to the employee and appropriate for her to do in her circumstances, and the terms and conditions applicable must not be substantially less favourable to her than her ordinary terms and conditions of employment. If the employee accepts such an offer then she will work in the alternative employment until she can be returned to her normal job. If she unreasonably declines to do the work she cannot be dismissed but she can then be suspended without pay.

If no suitable alternative employment can be offered or if such employment is offered but reasonably refused by the employee, then she must be suspended on full pay. Strictly speaking what she would be entitled to would be a statutory 'week's pay' in respect of each week of her absence as defined in Schedule 14 to the 1978 Act. It should be noted that the statutory maximum on a week's pay for some purposes does not apply for this purpose, so for most employees the entitlement will be normal full pay.

Return to work part-time after maternity

Many women would like to return to work part-time or, if already working part-time, for fewer hours per week. There is no statutory entitlement to return to anything other than the job which the women previously held. Under section 6 of the GWC Conditions of Service, Health Service employers are asked wherever possible to meet the expectation of women wanting to return under more flexible working arrangements. This provision arguably creates a contractual obligation upon employers operating Whitley Council maternity leave to seek to arrange part-time work or a job share if possible.

There is one other legal consideration which is the Sex Discrimination Act. Under that Act women must not be treated less favourably than men would be in similar circumstances. Therefore, if a women can satisfy a Tribunal that a man who had wanted to work part-time or more flexibly would have been treated more favourably, she is entitled to a finding of sex discrimination with appropriate compensation.

Having set out the legal background, it is worth commenting that there are many human resource management reasons for an employer to seek to accommodate the special needs of women with young children in relation to working arrangements. Even if return to the employee's former job on a part-time basis cannot be arranged, it may well be possible to find other work that would be acceptable to the employee and which the employer can offer. It is vital that both the employer and the employee are frank and open with each other about such possibilities. An employee who has taken maternity leave and arranged her life on the basis of indications that a part-time return would be, or might be, allowed, is entitled to feel aggrieved (and may well have a legal claim) if she is subsequently disappointed. Unless a definite arrangement has been made, it is therefore important that any communications with an employee about the possibility of part-time work make it absolutely clear that no guarantees are being given.

Maternity pay

Any maternity pay to a woman made under the Whitley Council conditions or alternative contractual arrangements counts towards statutory maternity pay. Statutory maternity pay is the absolute minimum and after being paid cannot be recouped even if the woman does not intend to return to work – indeed a woman who has conclusively decided when she leaves to have the baby that she will not return to work is still entitled to statutory maternity pay.

However, so far as the surplus of pay over statutory maternity pay is concerned, section 6 of the GWC Conditions of Service does contain some special rules. First of all, if she does not intend to return to work with her employer or any other Health Service employer then she is entitled only to statutory maternity pay. Secondly, if she received contractual maternity pay but then did not return to work with her existing employer or another Health Service employer then she must repay any contractual maternity pay. It is not clear from the relevant paragraph in the section 6 of the GWC Conditions of Service whether her return to work must be within 12 months or 15 months.

CHAPTER 4

DISCRIMINATION

INTRODUCTION

All employers are required to provide equal opportunities for employees, regardless of sex or ethnic origin, by ensuring that there is no discrimination within the working environment against employees. The Sex Discrimination Act 1975 ('SDA') established the Equal Opportunities Commission ('EOC') to:

(a) work towards the elimination of discrimination;

(b) promote equality of opportunity between men and women generally; and

(c) keep under review the working of the SDA and the Equal Pay Act 1970 and to draw up proposals for amendments from time to time.

In addition, the EOC has the power to issue codes of practice which, although not legally binding, may be taken into account by an Industrial Tribunal. The Race Relations Act 1976 ('RRA') established the Commission for Racial Equality ('CRE'), that has similar functions to the EOC.

Discrimination legislation gives potentially far wider protection than unfair dismissal legislation. There are no restrictions in relation to qualifying periods of service for employees to bring a claim, that contrasts with the legislation relating to unfair dismissal rights under the Employment Protection (Consolidation) Act 1978 ('EPCA'). In addition, for the purposes of the SDA and the RRA, the definition of 'employment' includes self-employed persons provided their contract requires them to execute their work personally (SDA section 82(1); RRA section 78(1)). Further, whilst the EPCA provides limited protection in relation to unfair dismissal, the SDA and the RRA protect the employee in every part of the employment relationship from recruitment, appointment, promotion, dismissal and the provision of benefits. In addition, the RRA and SDA extend to the provision of services which is far wider than the EPCA, that only protects 'employees'.

Section 50 Whitley Council in relation to development of Retainer Schemes specifically stresses:

'the importance of health authorities, operating an equal opportunities policy in employment irrespective of age, gender, marital status, race, religion, creed, sexual orientation, colour or disability.'

This statement arguably widens the principles of equal opportunities to categories not currently covered by the discrimination legislation. However, employers are advised that to ignore such principles will be at their peril as, even if the UK does not at present specifically outlaw discrimination on the grounds of say, age or sexuality, it is likely that Europe will dictate that to so discriminate will be in breach of European Directives on equality of treatment.

DEFINITION

There are three types of discrimination covered by the SDA and the RRA and these are as follows:

- direct discrimination;

- indirect discrimination;

- victimisation.

Direct discrimination

The SDA outlaws direct discrimination against men, women and married persons on the grounds of sex or marital status. Section 1(1)(a) of the SDA provides that:

'A person discriminates against a woman in any circumstances relevant to the purposes of any provision of this Act if:

On the grounds of her sex he treats her less favourably than he treats or would treat a man.'

Section 3(1)(a) refers to direct discrimination against married persons where:

'On the grounds of his or her marital status he treats that person less favourably than he treats or would treat an unmarried person of the same sex.'

The definition of direct discrimination in the RRA is virtually identical to that in the SDA, however, obviously it is based on racial grounds. Section 1(1)(a) of the RRA provides that direct discrimination occurs where:

'On racial grounds he treats or would treat that other person less favourably than he treats or would treat other persons.'

Racial grounds is defined in section 3 of the RRA as:

'Colour, race, nationality, ethnic or national origins.'

Indirect discrimination

Under the SDA indirect discrimination occurs where:

'He applies a requirement or condition which he applies or would equally apply to a man but:

1   which is such that the proportion of women who could comply with it is considerably smaller than the proportion of men who could comply with it; and

2   which he cannot show to be justifiable in respect of the sex of the person to whom it is applied; and

3   which is to her detriment because she cannot comply with it.'

The RRA has equivalent provisions relating to indirect discrimination.

From the definitions above, it can be seen that direct discrimination is the most obvious and easily identifiable form of discrimination. It is where a person is treated differently by reason of race, sex or marital status and such treatment is less favourable than that person would otherwise have received. It does not matter that the motive for the less favourable treatment is non-discriminatory. The important fact is the impact of the treatment.

The 'But For' test

The distinction between motive and reason is illustrated by the House of Lords case of *James v Eastleigh Borough Council* (1990).[1] In that case Eastleigh Borough Council had set different age limits for men and women for concessionary rates at the Borough Swimming Pool and local amenities. Their motive for doing so was to provide subsidies to perceived needs and it was administratively convenient to relate this to the state pensionable age. The House of Lords concluded that the reason for the treatment was the sex of the Applicant and consequently he had a legitimate claim. They laid down the 'but for' test for determining whether there had been direct discrimination. The test is therefore as follows:

'Would the complainant have received the same treatment from the defendant but for his or her sex?'

The motive behind the discriminatory treatment is irrelevant.

In deciding whether or not there has been indirect discrimination, a number of questions have to be considered, these are:

• Is there a condition or requirement?

• Is the condition or requirement absolute? If the condition or requirement is not absolute but is preferred or desirable, then it will not constitute indirect discrimination;

• Is it applied universally?

• Has the applicant established her sex, marital status or racial grouping?

---

[1]   [1990] ICR 554.

- Has the applicant established that the condition was applied to her detriment?

- Can the applicant or person of the same sex, marital status or racial group comply?

- Is there a disproportionate impact?

- Can the requirement be otherwise justified irrespective of sex, race or marital status? If not, indirect discrimination will exist.

EMPLOYERS LIABILITY

Under the principle of vicarious liability, employers are liable for the acts of their employees that are carried out in the course of their employment. Conversely, where acts are outside the scope of the employment, the employer will not be liable.

So, for example, in *Irving v Post Office* (1987)[2] the Post Office were not vicariously liable under the Race Relations Act for racially abusive words written on the back of an envelope by a postman, since the postman was not acting in the course of his employment. The act of writing on the envelope did not become part of the manner in which the postman performed his duties merely because he did it whilst on duty. His employment provided the opportunity for his misconduct but the misconduct itself formed no part of the performance of his duties, was in no way directed towards the performance of those duties, and was not done for the benefit of his employer.

The employer's statutory defence

Section 41(3) of the SDA and section 32(3) of the RRA provide that if the employer took such steps as were reasonably practicable to prevent the employee from doing a discriminatory act, then the employer would not be vicariously liable. The onus is on the employer to establish that he has taken such steps as are reasonably practicable. In *Balgobin v London Borough of Tower Hamlet* (1987),[3] the Industrial Tribunal held that the respondents had a defence under section 41(3) of the SDA to acts of sexual harassment committed by their employee, by establishing that they 'took such steps as were reasonably practicable to prevent the employee from doing' the acts complained of in circumstances in which the allegations had not been made known to management; that there was proper and adequate staff supervision; and that the employers had made known their policy of equal opportunities.

---

[2] [1987] IRLR 289.

[3] [1987] IRLR 401 EAT.

It is clear that measures such as training for those in supervisory positions and the implementation of an Equal Opportunities Policy as well as the compliance with the EOC or CRE code of practice will assist an employer in avoiding liability. The failure to follow the EOC or CRE codes of practice does not, of itself, render an employer liable to proceedings. However, the codes are admissible in evidence and would assist an employer in showing that he took such steps as were reasonably practicable to prevent employees from doing the act in question or acts of that description.

PRE-EMPLOYMENT DISCRIMINATION

Recruitment

Section 6(1) of the SDA provides that:

'It is unlawful for a person in relation to employment by him if, at an establishment in Great Britain, to discriminate against a woman:

(a) in the arrangements he makes for the purpose of determining who should be offered that employment; or

(b) the terms on which he offers her that employment; or

(c) by refusing or deliberately omitting to offer her that employment.'

Accordingly, this section provides that it is unlawful to discriminate against individuals in all aspects of the recruitment procedure including advertising, short-listing criteria, short-listing process, interviewing and selection. If a woman who is not appointed to a position appears, on paper, to be better qualified or suited to the post than the successful male applicant, the employer may be called upon to provide a satisfactory explanation for the apparent discrimination. The SDA covers omissions as well as actions, so that a failure to advertise a vacancy may in some circumstances constitute indirect discrimination until and unless it can be justified. Identical provisions are contained in the RRA.

Advertising

By virtue of section 38 of the SDA the EOC has the power to prosecute advertisers and publishers of discriminatory advertisements.

Section 38 provides that it is unlawful to advertise a position in a manner which restricts those who could apply or those who can be appointed by virtue of sex or marital status. Advertising includes internal advertising or staff notices and possibly even word of mouth.

This provision will, therefore, also apply to internal newsletters regarding promotion opportunities. Section 38(3) specifically provides that the use of terms with a sexual connotation such as 'waiter', 'salesgirl', 'postman' or 'stewardess' will be taken to indicate an intention to discriminate unless there is an indication to the contrary.

This provision can only be enforced by the EOC and is limited to a declaration by a Tribunal that discrimination occurred, or an injunction restraining further such acts. Section 29 of the RRA contains similar provisions. In this case, the prosecuting body is the CRE.

In certain circumstances, advertisements may be permitted to be discriminatory. These are as follows:

- for jobs where sex, race, colour, ethnic or national origin is a genuine occupational qualification (see below);

- under statutory authority eg a navigation order 1985 which states that a pregnant woman may not work as a flight crew;

- for advertising positions or training within the company, where the employer has identified that (in the past 12 months) there were no individuals of a particular sex or racial group (or a disproportionate number) doing that particular job or type of job (SDA section 48; RRA section 37). In effect this provision allows some positive discrimination but it does not allow an employer to discriminate in respect of the actual appointment itself;

- for advertising a job or training opportunity outside the work place to groups defined by sex or race. The employer must have identified that (in the past 12 months) there were none or a disproportionate number of individuals of one sex doing one job or type of job in the UK as a whole, or in that area of the country. Again this does not justify discrimination in the actual appointment (SDA section 38, 47(1)(2); RRA section 29, 37(1)(2));

- for advertising posts where a condition or requirement indirectly discriminates but which can be justified irrespective of sex or race;

- where the employment is for religious purposes and the employment is limited to one sex for doctrinal reasons (SDA section 19, 38(2));

- where the advertisement indicates that persons of any class defined other than by reference to colour, ethnic or national origins are required for employment outside the UK (RRA section 29(3), eg English persons to teach English abroad, English nanny);

The EOCs code of practice provides guidance on non-discriminatory advertising. Its recommendations include the following:

- that job advertising should be carried out in such a way to encourage applications from suitable candidates of either sex (both in terms of wording and in the publications in which they are placed);

- that advertising material should be reviewed in order to ensure that it avoids stereotyping men and women;

- that where vacancies are filled by promotion or transfer, they should be advertised to all eligible employees and should not be advertised in such a way that they restrict applications from one sex;

- recruitment solely or primarily by word of mouth should be avoided where the workforce is predominantly of one sex, as this may unnecessarily restrict the choice of applications;

- similarly, where applicants are supplied through Trade Union and members of one sex only come forward, this should be discussed with the Unions and an alternative approach adopted.

The CREs code of practice advises employers 'not to confine recruitment unjustifiably to those agencies, job centres, careers offices and schools which, because of their particular source of applicants, provide only or mainly applications of a particular racial group'.

Application forms

Again, application forms should not demonstrate any race or sex bias and should be as comprehensive as possible. Accordingly, discriminatory questions should be avoided at all costs. Examples of such questions are those relating to marital or family commitments if they are asked of one sex only. In any event, there is a risk that such questions, even if asked of both sexes, are construed as showing a bias against female candidates. Application forms should be processed in exactly the same way and information necessary for personnel records can be collected after a job offer has been made. It is therefore recommended that a separate set of questions for equal opportunities monitoring is issued to applicants as a separate document and that the candidate is left in no doubt that the information collated from that form will in no way have any effect on the eventual selection of the successful candidate.

Criteria for shortlisting

Obviously it will be direct discrimination to fail to short list candidates because of their race, sex or marital status. However, there are less obvious criteria which may constitute indirect discrimination and which could not be justified on a non-sexual or non-racial ground. For example, requirements to have particular supervisory experience may be discriminatory as against women if those requirements are linked to a maximum age requirement for the post. This is because it is likely that statistically it could be shown that women are more likely to take a career break for family reasons rather than men. Consequently, job criteria should be carefully considered and, if at all possible, the criteria should be a desirable rather than an essential requirement. Only if the criteria are requirements will they constitute indirect discrimination.

Interviews

Again, employers must ensure that where selection is based on an interview, those involved in the decision-making process should not take decisions that are discriminatory against interviewees on grounds of race, sex or marital status.

The EOC and CRE recommend that all staff involved in the interviewing process are trained in the provisions of the SDA and the RRA and of the dangers of making stereotype assumptions on the basis of race, sex or marital status. In addition, all applications should be processed in an identical way as indicated above and the EOC and CRE recommend that there should not be separate lists of applicants based on gender and/or race. Interviews should be carefully recorded so that in the event of claims being brought against the employer for failure to appoint, the employer has an accurate record of what was said that would help to assist in defending such a claim. Ideally, the record of the interview should also contain a note of the reasons why the particular applicant was or was not selected.

Where the job involves unsocial hours or extensive travel, it may be necessary to assess whether personal circumstances will affect the individual's performance. If this is the case, the EOC code states that such issues should be discussed objectively without detailed questioning based on assumptions about marital status, children or domestic obligations. The code points out that any information that is necessary for personnel records can be collected after a job offer has been made.

Genuine occupational qualifications

Both the RRA and the SDA provide limited circumstances in which it is lawful to discriminate because of a Genuine Occupational Qualification (GOQ). Thus, where the sex or race of an employee is a GOQ for the post in question and:

- the employer discriminates against a prospective employee in the arrangements he makes for filling the job; or

- the employer discriminates against a prospective employee by refusing her the job; or

- the employer denies an employee the opportunities for promotion, transfer or training for the job in question.

The list of GOQs within the RRA and the SDA are exhaustive, so that if a reason does not fall within one of the categories as specified there will not be a valid defence. The GOQs can apply even if only part of the job relates to the GOQ criteria, as the legislation refers to 'some of the duties' which does not impose a fixed proportion.

GOQs (sex)

The following are GOQs that apply in respect of sex discrimination only.

Decency or privacy

A GOQ will exist if a job needs to be held by one particular sex in order to preserve decency or privacy. Section 7(2) of the SDA provides as follows:

'(b) The job needs to be held by a man to preserve decency or privacy because:

i   it is likely to involve physical contact with men in circumstances where they might reasonably object to it being carried out by a woman; or

ii the holder of the job is likely to do his work in circumstances where men might reasonably object to the presence of a woman, because they are in a state of undress or are using sanitary facilities.'

Accordingly this exception would apply to swimming pool changing room attendants, toilet attendants etc.

Domestic staff

Where the employee is working or living in a private home in which the individual has close physical or social contact with a person living in that home or knowledge of intimate or personal details of the employer, then again, the GOQ will exist. Such employees might be live-in nurses or domestic staff.

Single sex sleeping and toilet facilities

There will be a GOQ where the employee has live-in premises provided by his or her employer and:

'(i) The only such premises which are available for persons holding that kind of job are lived in or normally lived in by men and are not equipped with separate sleeping accommodation for women and sanitary facilities which could be used by women in privacy from men; and

(ii) It is not reasonable to expect the employer either to equip those premises with such accommodation and facilities or to provide other premises for women.'

This provision covers live-in employees such as lighthouse keepers and caretakers where the nature or location of the job makes it impracticable to live elsewhere, there is no separate sleeping and sanitary accommodation and it is not reasonable for the employer to make alternative arrangements to provide such accommodation. The provision places a burden on an employer on the question of reasonableness and accordingly employers should be careful to ensure that they consider the practicability of providing such alternative arrangements if they are to rely on this defence.

Single sex establishments

Where there are single sex institutions such as hospitals, prisons, children's and old people's homes, there may be a GOQ. Section 7(2)(d) provides that there will be a GOQ where:

'The nature of the establishment, or part of it within which the work is done, requires the job to be held by a man because:

i   it is, or is part of, a hospital, prison or other establishment for persons requiring special care, supervision or attention; and

ii   those persons are all men (disregarding any women whose presence is exceptional); and

iii it is reasonable, having regard to the essential character of the establishment or that part, that the job should not be held by a woman.'

This is a wide ranging provision that turns on the question as to whether or not it is reasonable that the job is held by somebody who is of the same sex as the inmates or residents. As with other cases, the defence will not succeed where there is evidence that the job has not, in the past, been exclusive to one sex.

Employment outside the UK

Being a man is a GOQ if the job is:

'likely to involve the performance of duties outside the United Kingdom in a country whose laws or customs are such that the duties could not, or could not effectively, be performed by a woman.' (SDA section 7(2)(g))

Married couples

Section 7(2)(h) of the SDA (1975) provides that being a man/woman is a GOQ where a 'job is one of two to be held by a married couple'. So, for example, the positions of housekeeper and gardener or head groom and cook would fall within this category.

GOQs (race and sex)

The following is a list of GOQs that apply both to race and sex cases.

Authenticity

This applies where physiology is the essential nature of the job. The exception applies to models etc and employers must disregard actual physical strength or stamina. Alternatively, where a dramatic performance requires an individual of a particular sex or race for purposes of authenticity, then it would be permissible to make such a requirement (SDA section 7(2)(a) and RRA section 5(2)(a)).

Personal welfare services

This applies where the job involves the provision of personal services promoting welfare, education, or similar services and that can most effectively be done by an individual of a particular race or sex. Accordingly this exclusion can cover social workers, teachers, nurses etc in certain circumstances. For example, a black, male AIDS worker might be legitimate provided that the employer could show that the significant proportion of the client group were black and male and that their personal welfare needs could most effectively be provided by a black, male worker.

GOQ (race only)

The only GOQ peculiar to race is employment in an ethnic restaurant and is often known as the 'Chinese Restaurant Exception'. It allows racial groups to be specified for authenticity reasons.

DISCRIMINATION DURING EMPLOYMENT

Once the employment relationship has commenced, then both the SDA and RRA set out what acts of discrimination are unlawful. The Acts provide that it is unlawful for an employer to discriminate against employees in the following situations:

- by restricting or denying access to promotion, transfer or training;
- by restricting or denying access to any other benefits, facilities or services;
- by dismissal;
- by subjecting them to any detriment.

Promotion

Both the SDA and the RRA provide that equal opportunities to promotion must be provided regardless of race or sex. Complaints about failure to obtain promotion are fairly common and, bearing in mind that inevitably the employment relationship continues whilst the complaint is processed, the claims can prove to be extremely stressful for all those involved. Employers should be aware in particular that although it is rare that there will be overt direct discrimination in denying access to promotion, often there are subconscious prejudices exercised by interviewers which are highlighted when statistically it is shown that the particular interviewer has failed to promote a significant proportion of the sex or race involved. In *West Midlands Passenger Transport Executive v Singh* (1988),[4] the Court of Appeal highlighted the problems of attempting to appoint individuals on an objective basis. The Court recognised that the suitability of candidates could rarely be measured objectively and often required subjective judgment. Consequently, it held that evidence of a high percentage rate of failure to achieve promotion at a particular levels by members of a particular racial group, may indicate that the real reason for refusal was a conscious or unconscious racial attitude that involved stereotyped assumptions about members of that group.

The Equal Opportunities Commission Code section 24 recommends that assessment criteria should be monitored to ensure a non-discriminatory application and that career development patterns should be reviewed regularly to ensure that there is no unlawful indirect discrimination. However, in order for indirect discrimination to be made out, it is necessary for the requirement or condition to be an absolute bar. It is not enough that the criteria is one of many that are weighed up in deciding who should or should

---

[4]   [1988] IRLR 186.

not be appointed. In *Perera v Civil Service Commission* (1983),[5] the Court of Appeal suggested that a 'requirement or condition' meant something that had to be complied with in the sense that the lack of compliance would be an absolute bar.

Restrictions on transfer

This may amount to indirect discrimination if the pool from which transfers are restricted is made up of mainly female or minority groups. In *Frances v British Aerospace Engineering Overhaul Limited* (1982),[6] the Employment Appeal Tribunal held that indirect discrimination would be made out where a requirement for transfer is the membership of a particular class or group of employees and that class or group has a predominance of one sex.

Restrictions on training

The EOC recommend that policies and practices regarding selection for training, day release and personal development should be examined for unlawful direct or indirect discrimination. Where there is found to be an imbalance in training as between sexes, the cause should be identified to ensure that it is not discriminatory. For example, if training facilities are only provided during the evenings and weekends, these may be indirectly discriminatory against one sex by reason of family commitments. It would therefore be for the employer to show that it had some objective justification for providing the training at those times with reference to the cost and convenience to the employer. The Tribunal would then have to balance the discriminatory effect against those objective criteria in deciding whether or not discrimination had occurred.

Exceptions for positive encouragement and training

The RRA and the SDA do provide exceptions for employers to take positive action steps in respect of training. For example, training boards, employers and Trade Unions may discriminate in training and employ encouraging advertising, if during the 12 months preceding that training there were:

- no persons of that gender/race doing the job; or

- where there is under representation of ethnic minorities or a particular gender in a particular grade.

---

5   [1983] IRLR 166.

6   [1982] IRLR EAT 10.

Training bodies may favour persons who are in special need of training because of domestic or family responsibilities having excluded them from regular full time employment. This particularly affects mothers returning to work. Finally, Trade Unions may reserve seats on elected bodies and organise discriminatory recruitment campaigns if during the preceding 12 months the organisation has had no women members.

Facilities and benefits

It is unlawful to discriminate on grounds of race or sex in the provision of any other benefits such as private health, company car, sick pay etc, unless they are benefits given to a woman in connection with pregnancy or childbirth. Section 2(2) of the SDA prevents men from complaining about the special treatment to women in connection with childbirth and pregnancy and as such access to ante-natal care, maternity leave and return to work provisions are all covered.

Conversely, it may be open for women who are absent on maternity leave to complain that they have been discriminated against if they are not given equal access to benefits during maternity leave as a comparable male if he were sick. This argument is before the European Court of Justice at the time of writing with the cases of *Todd v Eastern Health and Social Security Board*[7] and *Gillespie v Eastern Health and Social Security Services Board* (1991). In those cases it was argued that the amount of contractual maternity pay should be at least as good as that of contractual sick pay.

It should be noted that the access to 'facilities' has been interpreted by the Employment Appeal Tribunal as meaning facilities that already exist. Consequently there is no obligation on an employer to create additional facilities. In *Clymo v London Borough of Wandsworth* (1989)[8] the appellant could not complain that her employers refusal to allow her to share her job was discriminatory, since the employer did not allow anyone to job share and consequently job sharing was not an existing facility.

Mobility clauses

The inclusion of a mobility clause in contracts of employment has long been a cause of disquiet within both Courts and Tribunals. Arguments put forward in support of employers relying on mobility clauses – particularly in redundancy situations – have not always found favour.

The Court of Appeal was recently requested to make a ruling on whether such a mobility clause constituted indirect discrimination. The clause in

---

[7] Case 11/49/99EP.
[8] [1989] IRLR 241.

question required the employee to 'serve in such parts of the UK ... as the Council may ... require'. Under section 77 of the Sex Discrimination Act 1975, an employee can challenge an employment contract or any particular provision contained in it on the grounds that it is discriminatory and contrary to the Act. In *Mead-Hill & Another v The British Council*[9], the Court of Appeal decided that a mobility clause could be more of a burden to female employees. The Court expressed its concern that it may amount to indirect discrimination on the grounds that fewer women would be able to comply with the requirement that might be made for them to move their base of work.

The Court has not ruled the clause unlawful, but the Council must now go back to the High Court justifying its inclusion. What is clear, is that employers must consider the effect of inserting a mobility clause and be able to justify its inclusion. An organisation must be able to establish the need to have flexibility and mobility.

Dismissal

It is unlawful to dismiss an employee by reason of sex or race (RRA section 4(2)(c); SDA section 6(2)(b)). In particular redundancy criteria should be examined to ensure that they are not discriminatory. For example, where 'last in first out' ('LIFO') criteria are used, these may be both indirectly racially or sexually discriminatory. Equally, where part-timers are automatically selected before full timers for redundancy, this would almost certainly be discriminatory following the House of Lords decision in March 1994 of *R v Secretary of State for Employment, ex parte Equal Opportunities Commission* where the Commission established that proportionally more women worked part-time than men.

It should be noted that refusing to accept discriminatory instructions resulting in an employees dismissal, would also be direct discrimination. For example, that the employer should refuse to provide services to a particular racial group (see *Zarczynska v Levy* (1979)[10]).

Constructive dismissal

If an individual can show that his or her employer is in a repudiatory breach of contract, then he or she would be able to terminate his or her contract of employment and claim that he or she has been constructively dismissed. Accordingly, where the employer has been discriminating against the employee by reason of sexual or racial harassment, the employee who terminates the contract would be able to claim that the reason for the dismissal was discriminatory and that it related to the acts of harassment.

---

9   [1995] *The Times* 14 April.

10   [1979] ICR 184.

VICTIMISATION

After direct and indirect discrimination, victimisation is the third form of discrimination recognised by the RRA and the SDA. The aim of the provisions relating to victimisation are to prevent individuals from being penalised for pursuing their rights, or supporting others, under the legislation. The statutory definition of victimisation is found in section 4(1) of the SDA and section 2(1) of the RRA. These provide that victimisation will occur if a person ('the discriminator') treats another person ('the person victimised') less favourably than another person, and does so because the person victimised has asserted his/her rights or assisted others in one of the ways defined in this section. These are referred to as the 'protected acts' and are as follows:

- brought proceedings against the discriminator or any other person under the relevant employment protection legislation; or

- given evidence or information in connection with proceedings brought by a person against the discriminator or any other person under the relevant employment legislation; or

- otherwise done anything under or by reference to the relevant Act in relation to the discriminator or any other person; or

- alleged that the discriminator or any other person has committed an act which (whether or not the allegation states) would amount to a contravention of the relevant employment protection legislation.

The sections also protect those who intend to do any of the protected acts or who are suspected to have done so or suspected of intending to do so.

Generally individuals are not protected if the original allegations were false and they were not made in good faith. However, employers should be wary of relying on these provisions, as it is always difficult to establish that an individual was acting in bad faith and an Industrial Tribunal would have to make an express finding of bad faith or untruthfulness in order for reliance to be placed on this.

As stated above, the applicant must establish that there was 'less favourable treatment'. Obviously that treatment will be shown to exist if the individual has been dismissed or demoted, however, there is often more petty treatment that can amount to 'less favourable treatment' within the meaning of the relevant provisions. In *Blair v Nottingham Flow Controls*[11] the less favourable treatment was the allowing of a less flexible lunch hour than other employees. In addition, the employee in question had received a memorandum in more forceful terms to her than to other employees. These actions were held to be as a direct result of the individual serving a sex discrimination questionnaire on the respondent.

---

[11] (COIT 01446/89).

Secondly, it must be established that the less favourable treatment was afforded to the employee in question 'by reason that' she had taken steps in proceedings under the relevant employment protection Act. Employers often fall into the trap of taking disciplinary action or treating employees to their detriment, due to the fact that they have been guilty of 'whistle blowing'. Often an employer will be quick to state that the reason the less favourable treatment has been afforded to the employee was not due to the fact that they had instigated proceedings under the relevant act, but instead that they had disclosed confidential information to a third party.

The Court of Appeal in *Aziz v Trinity Street Taxis* (1988)[12] has made it clear that where an individual has been afforded special treatment due to the fact that he has done one of the protected acts, then invariably that will be enough to prove victimisation. Accordingly, employers should ensure that employees are made aware of the possibility of victimisation claims and that even where an individual has lost a claim under one of the relevant acts, the staff are made aware that the applicant is not treated differently and is subject to normal treatment in the work place.

PART-TIME EMPLOYEES

Since the vast majority of part-time employees are women, if they are subject to any detriment by reason of their part-time status, this may be indirect discrimination, unless it can be justified, irrespective of sex. The European Court of Justice has held that the justification must 'relate to a real need on the part of the undertaking, and be appropriate with a view to achieving the objectives pursued and be necessary to that end' (*Bilka-Kaufhaus GmbH v Weber Von Hartz* (1980)[13]).

In March 1994 the House of Lords delivered a surprising decision upholding a challenge by the EOC to the law on redundancy payments that has been in existence since the Industrial Relations Act 1971. The House of Lords stated that the provisions in UK law that provide for employees working between eight and 16 hours per week obtaining their rights to redundancy payment on termination of employment by reason of redundancy, were discriminatory and contrary to the EC measures in relation to equal treatment.

The basis of the EOCs case was that part-time employees do not have the same employment rights as their full time colleagues, and in view of the fact that the vast majority of part-time employees are women, this amounted to sex discrimination. The decision was a declaration meaning that it was merely

---

[12] [1988] IRLR 204.
[13] [1980] IRLR 317.

a statement of the House of Lords view of the law and did not actually change existing UK law as far as private employers are concerned. Nevertheless, following from the decision Industrial Tribunals applied their own interpretation, so for example, in *Warren v Wylie and Wylie* the Southampton Industrial Tribunal held that all employees with two years continuous service with their employer, had the right to complain of unfair dismissal regardless of the hours worked and regardless of whether their employer was in the public or private sector.

Consequently, the UK Government has now repealed all provisions in employment legislation relating to hourly thresholds by virtue of the Employment Protection (Part-time employees) Regulations 1995, which came into force on 6 February 1995.

HOMOSEXUALITY

There is no express legislation providing protection for homosexual individuals in employment and case law has tended to suggest that an employee, dismissed for what his or her employer perceives to be a consequence of their sexual preferences, stands little chance of success in an unfair dismissal claim. For example in *Saunders v Scottish National Camps* (1980),[14] the applicant was a groundsman at a children's holiday camp. When his employers became aware of his homosexuality and of his involvement in a sexual incident in a nearby town, they dismissed him. Apparently the employers feared that some of the children's parents might feel anxiety if they knew of the applicant's employment at the camp. The Employment Appeal Tribunal held that, if a considerable proportion of employers would take the view that the employment of a homosexual would be restricted where the work involved proximity to children, then, regardless of whether or not this was a valid view to be held, the dismissal could be lawful.

Again, in the case of *Buck v The Letchworth Palace*, the EAT held in 1987 that, where the applicant had been convicted of soliciting in a public lavatory, and fellow employees had told their employer that they no longer wished to work with him due to health fears, the ensuing dismissal was fair. The rational behind these decisions seems to be that the reason for the dismissal falls within the 'some other substantial reason' definition as provided in section 57 of the EPCA. The courts have been quick to stress that it is not the actual sexuality of the individual that is the reason for the dismissal but, instead, it is the fact that other employees at the employer's place of work refuse to work with the individual.

---

[14] [1980] IRLR 174.

In the recent case of *Regina v Ministry of Defence ex parte Smith & Others*[15], the applicants were all members of the Armed Forces who were dismissed due to their sexual orientation, but their applications were refused for, amongst other things, certioriari to quash decisions to dismiss them from the Armed Forces. They were also refused declarations that the policy of the Secretary of State was unlawful.

However, the Law Lords did state in their judgments that it was the very fact that service men and women had to hide their sexual orientation that left them exposed to the threat of blackmail. Furthermore, Lord Justice Simon Brown also stated that in his view, having homosexuals in the Armed Forces would impair operational efficiency or fighting effectiveness.

Notwithstanding that individuals may not have a claim for unfair dismissal related to their sexuality, they may have a claim under the sex discrimination legislation. Section 1(1) of the SDA provides that it is unlawful to discriminate against an individual on the ground of their sex if they are treated less favourably than a member of the opposite sex is, or would be treated. The difficulty lies in the fact that the definition refers to sex and not sexuality. However, in *James v Eastleigh Borough Council* (1990)[16] the House of Lords held that the correct test under section 1 of the SDA was objective and not subjective. The case formulated the 'but for' test as discussed previously in this chapter.

This reasoning, if applied to cases of dismissal on the grounds of sexual orientation, could mean that individuals would have a claim of direct discrimination. For example, where a male individual is dismissed due to the fact that he is having a sexual relationship with another male, he would argue that 'but for the fact that I am a man I would not have been dismissed'.

Obviously the issues relating to homosexuality are difficult and, although not directly related, the European Court of Justice has been asked to adjudicate in the case of *PVS v Cornwall County Council* on the question of the rights of transsexuals. In that case the European Court has been asked whether the principle of equal treatment for men and women from the Equal Treatment Directive applies to gender reassignment. A decision is still awaited from the European Court at the time of writing. However, presumably if the European Court agrees that transsexuals are covered by the Equal Treatment Directive, then presumably the same principles could be applied to sexual orientation.

In any event, employers are advised as a matter of good industrial relations, to make specific reference in equal opportunities codes of practice, to the fact that they do not permit discrimination on the grounds of sexuality. Employers should also note that Whitley Council specifically emphasises the importance of non discrimination on grounds of sexual orientation.

---

15 (1995) *The Times Law Reports*, 13 June.

16 [1990] IRLR 288.

DISABILITY

Whitley Council affirms its commitment to non discrimination on grounds of disability at section 50. Currently, the Disability Discrimination Bill has passed the House of Commons Committee stage. It is anticipated that the bill will be enacted by the early part of autumn 1995.

At present the framework of the bill is in keeping with the existing discrimination legislation. In section 3(1) discrimination in recruitment and selection is dealt with:

Section 3(1) – it is unlawful for an employer to discriminate against a disabled person –

- in the arrangements which he makes for the purposes of determining to whom he should offer employment;
- in the terms in which he offers that person employment; or
- by refusing to offer, or deliberately not offering him employment.

Discrimination occurring during employment is dealt with in section 3(2):

Section 3(2) – it is unlawful for an employer to discriminate against a disabled person whom he employs –

- in the terms of employment which he affords him;
- in the opportunities which he affords him for promotion, transfer, training or receiving any other benefit;
- by refusing to afford him or deliberately not affording him, any such opportunity; or
- by dismissing him or submitting him to any other detriment.

The definition of disability in the Bill includes a person having a 'physical or mental impairment which has a substantial and long term adverse affect on his ability to carry out normal day to day activities'. It is clear that impairment is intended to be restricted to a clinically, well recognised illness and will not include personality disorders or merely anti-social behaviour and addictions. Furthermore, the impairment will need to affect the normal day to day activities of the individuals. Some grey areas may arise in relation to illnesses such as schizophrenia or epilepsy, as they do not necessarily affect the normal day to day activities of the individual, but tend to cause problems intermittently. However, the impairment must have a 'long term effect', this is defined as an impairment which has lasted at least 12 months, or which can reasonably be expected to last for 12 months. It should be noted that persons with severe disfigurement are also covered by the Bill.

Employees and individuals who are currently registered as disabled under the provisions of the Disabled Persons (Employment) Act 1994, will remain automatically protected under the provisions of the Bill. This protection will last for a period of three years from the date that the Bill becomes enacted. After a three year period, these individuals will then have to satisfy the definition of disability in the Bill.

The definition of discrimination, in section 4 defines discrimination as where an employer discriminates against a disabled person:

- for a reason which relates to the disabled person's disability and who treats him less favourably than he treats or would treat others who do not have a disability; and

- the employer cannot show that the treatment in question is justified under section 5.

As this wording suggests, there are defences available. Section 5 states that:

There is no discrimination on grounds of disability where:

- in the employer's opinion, one or more of the conditions mentioned in subsection 4 are satisfied; and

- it is reasonable in all the circumstances of the case for him to hold that opinion.

The conditions contained in subsection 4 are:

- a disabled person is unsuitable for the employment;

- a disabled person is less suitable for the employment than another person, and that other person is given the employment;

- the nature of the disabled person's disability significantly impedes or would significantly impede, the performance of any of his duties; or

- in the case of training, the nature of the disabled person's disability will significantly reduce the value of the training (either to him or to the employer).

This is an exhaustive list, no other conditions are applicable. It should also be noted that the test focuses on the reasonable belief of the employer, unlike other areas of discrimination, it is a subjective test. The employer is under an obligation to show that in his opinion one of the exemptions is applicable. His opinion must be reasonable. Reasonableness will be defined within the principles laid out in British Leyland UK v Swift,[17] as being one of a band of reasonable responses within which 'one employer might reasonably take one view and another, quite reasonably, take another'.

---

17 (1981) IRLR 91.

A further defence is available in relation to section 6 of the Bill which requires employers to make adjustments to the workplace. Adjustments are required where a disabled person is placed at a substantial disadvantage as a job applicant or employee because of the arrangements or working conditions currently provided by the employer. A defence is afforded to any potential claim under these provisions if the employer can show that it was not reasonable to make such adjustments. The employer is under no general obligation to make adjustments and provide extensive access to disabled people in general, the duty is only owed to the individual disabled employee or job applicant. In considering the reasonableness of the adjustment, matters such as the financial cost, practicability and effectiveness will all be considered.

The Bill does not apply to businesses employing fewer than 20 employees. When calculating the number of employees there is no distinction drawn between part-time and full-time employees.

Disabled Persons (Registration) Regulations 1945

These provisions provide for a register of disabled persons to be maintained. This is kept by the Department of Employment and the entry shows that the person is both disabled within the definition of the Act and also capable of employment.

Disabled Persons (Employment) Act 1944

The Disabled Persons (Employment) Act 1944 ('DPA') imposes an obligation on all employers of 20 or more people to employ a quota of registered disabled persons. The Employment Protection (Consolidation) Act 1978, as amended, also protects all employees from being unfairly dismissed, subject to the qualifying period of two years continuous employment. Thus an individual could potentially have protection after the two year period against dismissal on arbitrary grounds of being disabled. However, it should be noted that one of the fair reasons for dismissal under the EPCA is capability, which covers dismissals on ill health grounds. As such, if the employer could show that the individual was no longer capable of carrying out his or her employment due to ill health, and a fair procedure had been followed in establishing this, then it is likely that the dismissal would be deemed to be fair within the meaning of section 57 of the EPCA.

The quota of registered disabled persons required to be employed under the DPA is currently 3%. However, an employer may apply to the Secretary of State for Employment for a reduced quota on the grounds that a 3% quota is too great in his particular circumstances. Where a redundancy situation occurs, then a disabled worker could potentially be given protection against redundancy on the grounds that if he were to be dismissed, then the company would have fallen below its 3% quota.

Failure to appoint a disabled person, or dismissing a disabled person without good cause where the number of disabled persons would fall below the quota, is a criminal offence carrying a level three fine or three months imprisonment. Proceedings are by summary trial in the Magistrates Court, however no proceedings may be brought without the consent of the Secretary of State. Consequently, in practice, it is extremely rare for proceedings to be brought and there have been only five convictions since 1961, the most recent in 1975.

It should be noted that if the Disability Discrimination Bill is enacted in its current form, the above provisions relating to quotas and criminal offences relating to failure to appoint will be repealed.

Code of practice

The Department of Employment has produced a code of practice on the employment of disabled persons. It is concerned with the employment of all disabled persons and covers:

- setting up policies on disabilities within an organisation;
- the law relating to employment of individuals with disabilities;
- characteristics of persons with disabilities and the consequences for employers;
- typical concerns of employers;
- good recruitment practice;
- options to consider for disabled persons;
- the role of employers and Trade Unions;
- a directory of sources of financial and other practical help available to assist in the employment of individuals with disabilities.

HARASSMENT

Harassment on the grounds of sex or race will constitute direct discrimination. The European Commission's Code of Practice for preventing and dealing with harassment at work describes sexual harassment as 'unwanted conduct of a sexual nature, or other conduct based on sex affecting the dignity of women and men at work'.

The Equal Opportunities Commission in its publication 'Sexual Harassment – What You Can Do About It' points out that sexual harassment includes behaviour such as comments about the way a woman looks, lewd remarks or glances, questions about a woman's sex life, requests for sexual favours, intimate physical contact or sexual assault. It is not necessary for there to be a series of incidents if one incident is sufficiently serious it can constitute sexual harassment.

The leading case of *Strathclyde Regional Council v Porcelli* (1986)[18] held that the objective of the harassers was not relevant to the issue of whether or not there had been sex discrimination in contravention of section 1 of the SDA, nor was it an acceptable argument that Mrs Porcelli had not been treated less favourably than an equally unpopular man. The point was that the weapon used against her was one that could only have been used against a woman and therefore she had been treated less favourably on the grounds of her sex.

Claims of sexual harassment can be brought against the harasser and against the employer. However, employers should be aware that one of the defences against vicarious liability is that the employer should have taken 'such steps as were reasonably practicable to prevent the employee from doing that Act, or from doing in the course of his employment, acts of that description' (SDA section 41(3); RRA section 32(3)). Accordingly, if employers have provided all employees with equal opportunities training and included in individuals contracts of employment that it would be a breach of contract to discriminate against fellow employees or members of the public on grounds of sex, race, sexuality or disability, then an initial defence could be set up under these sections.

QUESTIONNAIRE PROCEDURE

In addition to the normal rules applicable to Industrial Tribunal proceedings applying to sex discrimination or race discrimination cases, there are also specific provisions allowing individuals to serve a questionnaire on the respondents requesting information relevant to the proceedings. The questionnaire may be served by the applicant at any time before the proceedings and within 21 days after the issuing of proceedings. Although there is no strict legal obligation on the respondent to answer the questionnaire, if the respondents fail to answer questions put to it then the Industrial Tribunal may draw an adverse inference. The replies to the questionnaires are admissible in evidence at the Industrial Tribunal's proceedings.

The following remedies are available to the Industrial Tribunal where it makes a finding of discrimination:

---

[18]   [1986] IRLR 134.

- an order declaring the rights of the complainant and the respondent in relation to the action to which the complainant relates;

- an order requiring the respondent to pay the complainant compensation;

- a recommendation that the respondent takes action appearing to the tribunal to be practicable for the purpose of reducing the adverse affect on the complainant of any act or discrimination to which the complaint relates.

In practice the most common remedy is compensation. Unlike claims for unfair dismissal, there is now no limit on the amount to which an Industrial Tribunal can award a compensatory payment to an applicant and the MOD cases whereby individuals dismissed from the forces due to the fact that they were pregnant, have resulted in compensatory awards being made in the hundreds of thousands of pounds level. However, in the case of the *Ministry of Defence v Cannock and others* (1994),[19] the EAT gave guidance on how to assess compensation in pregnancy dismissal cases. The EAT held that the proper basis of calculating compensation was that of tort rather than contract, which means that damages should be assessed in putting the employee in the position they would have been if they had not been dismissed, but subject always to the duty to mitigate their loss.

REMEDIES FOR DISCRIMINATION AND HARASSMENT

All claims relating to discrimination in the employment field are made in the Industrial Tribunal. However, claims relating to discrimination falling outside the employment field are made in the County Court.

Industrial Tribunals hear applications relating to the following:

- claims under the Race Relations Act 1976;

- claims under the Sex Discrimination Act 1975;

- claims under the Equal Pay Act 1970;

- direct enforcement of the Treaty of Rome;

- proceedings brought by the EOC or CRE in respect of discriminatory advertisements;

- appeals against non-discrimination notices served by the EOC or CRE;

- unfair dismissal claims under the Employment Protection (Consolidation) Act 1978.

---

[19] [1994] IRLR 509.

There is no qualifying period for applications under the SDA or RRA and applications are made by the applicant submitting an Originating Application form IT1. The respondents will have 14 days from the receipt of the IT1 to form a Notice of Appearance form IT3. Either may apply to the other party for discovery of documents or may seek further and better particulars of the originating application or Notice of Appearance. In addition, either party may request the other party to reply to questions pertinent to the proceedings and the Tribunal may make an order in this regard if it considers that the answer to those questions may help to clarify issues likely to arise before determination in the proceedings and that it would be likely to assist the progress of the proceedings for that answer to be available to the Tribunal before the hearing.

Injury to feelings award

Industrial Tribunals may make an additional award to an applicant to reflect the injury she has suffered to her feelings. In *Noone v North West Thames Regional Council* (1988)[20] the Court of Appeal held that taking into account the limit in compensation at the time was £7,500 an award of £3,000 for injury to feelings was at the top end of the appropriate range for such awards. However, since the cap on discrimination awards has now been removed, it is questionable whether the guidance in *Noone* still applies.

According to a survey by the Equal Opportunities Review in 1994 the average award for injury to feelings in sex discrimination cases has increased by 35% since the cap has been removed and the average award for compensation for loss of earnings has also increased by 45% since removal of the cap.

Interest

Under the regulations that removed the cap from Industrial Tribunal awards for discrimination, Industrial Tribunals also have the power to award interest on compensatory awards. For loss of earnings interest is normally payable from the mid point to the period between the date of the actual discrimination complained of and the date the Tribunal calculates the interest.

Interest on injury to feelings awards, however, is awarded from the date of the act of discrimination.

---

[20] [1988] IRLR 195.

CHAPTER 5

EQUAL PAY

AIMS OF THE GOVERNING LEGISLATION

The Equal Pay Act 1970 ('EPA') is the governing legislation in UK law bringing into effect the provisions of the Equal Pay Directive and Article 119 of the Treaty of Rome ('Article 119'). The EPA therefore brings into force the principle that men and women should receive equal pay for equal work, being either the same work or work to which an equal value is attributed.

Although the EPA was passed in 1970 it did not become effective until 1975 as it is one of the core elements of the sex discrimination legislation and was brought into effect simultaneously with the Sex Discrimination Act 1975 ('SDA'). These two Acts are mutually exclusive but complimentary in that they aim to eliminate all discrimination on the grounds of sex in the work place. Together, they give employees the right to present complaints for unequal pay and for other discriminatory treatment at work.

SCOPE OF THE EQUAL PAY LEGISLATION

Section 1(1) of the EPA implies into every person's contract of employment, an 'equality clause' entitling that person to equal terms and conditions of employment to those of fellow employees of the opposite sex for doing the same sort of work, work rated as equivalent, or work of equal value. The effect of this implied clause is to upgrade any less favourable term in an employee's contract or to include in their contract a term corresponding to the more beneficial term in the employee's comparator's contract. The equality clause relates to all terms of the contract, whether concerned with pay or not. The courts have also interpreted the Act to enable a precise comparison of individual terms within employees contracts as opposed to comparing contracts as a whole (*Haywood v Camell Laird Ship Builders (No 2) (1988)*[1]).

---

[1] [1988] AC 894.

SIGNIFICANCE OF EU LAW

EU law so far as equal pay is concerned is of paramount importance, and indeed, most recent developments in this area of law emanate from the ECJs interpretation of Article 119, and the Equal Pay Directive, Article 119 provides that:

> 'Each Member State shall ... maintain the application of the principle that men and women should receive equal pay for equal work.'

Article 1(1) of the Equal Pay Directive states that:

> 'The principle of equal pay for men and women outlined in Article 119 of the Treaty ... means, for the same value or for work to which equal value is attributed, the elimination of all discrimination on grounds of sex with regard to all aspects and conditions of remuneration.'

Together, the Equal Pay Directive and Article 119 provides the basis of European Rights to Equal Pay. As a consequence, they are important because:

- They provide a minimum guarantee of the rights of individuals which should be available in Member States.

- Domestic law is increasingly being considered in the light of EU law that deals with the same subject matter, and very often, domestic law will be given a purposive construction, in order to ensure that it meets the intention of the drafters of EU legislation. Ambiguities are therefore resolved in favour of Article 119 or the Equal Pay Directive over domestic legislation.

- It would appear that Article 119 is directly effective in domestic law in equal value cases, and this is of particular importance if an argument is proved that the provisions of domestic law fall below the rights of Article 119, as it would appear that a right of action would be provided notwithstanding that there would not be one under domestic law.

- It is also possible for an individual to bring direct action for compensation against the State for failing to properly implement a Directive if the individual is injured by a Member State's failure to implement EU law correctly (see *Francovich and Bonifaci v Italy* (1992)[2]).

---

[2] [1992] IRLR 84.

THE DEFINITION OF 'PAY'

As mentioned above, the EPA is not only concerned with pay, but with all the terms of a contract of employment. However, pay is often what a particular applicant is anxious to increase, and so it is important to understand exactly what pay is. Existing case law has shown that pay under the EPA is broadly defined to include mortgage payments, bonuses, shift payments and overtime. Indeed, any remuneration obtained under a contract of employment may well fall to be considered as 'pay'.

It is also important to realise that the ECJ has gone on to give a broader and more purposive interpretation to the definition of 'pay' and has ruled that it covers the following benefits as well:

- Statutory Sick Pay;

- Compensation for unfair dismissal;

- Concessionary railway fares;

- Notional salary additions;

- Occupational pensions;

- Redundancy payments.

In other words, the ECJ has extended the meaning of pay to include certain payments outside the contract of employment itself.

TYPES OF CLAIMS UNDER THE EQUAL PAY ACT

Section 1(2) of the EPA creates three situations under which an employee can bring a claim. These are:

1   Where the employee is employed in like work with an employee of the opposite sex (EPA section 1(2)(a)), which means that their work is broadly of a similar nature and any differences in the duties the employees perform are of no practical importance in relation to the terms and conditions of the employment.

2   Where the employee is employed on work rated as equivalent with that of an employee of the opposite sex (EPA s 1(2)(b)), this means that the employees work has been rated as equivalent and their two jobs have been given an equal value in terms of the demand made upon each employee in a job evaluation study (taking into account the 'skill', 'effort' and 'decision-taking' involved).

3   Where the employee is employed on work which does not fall within (a) or (b) above, is, in terms of the demands made upon the employee (for example, under such headings as 'effort', 'skill' and 'decision making'), of equal value to that of an employee of the opposite sex in the same employment. If a claim is made under this comparison, the fact that the claimant may be employed doing the same work as an employee of the opposite sex on the same pay does not de-bar them from making a claim for equal value and choosing a different comparator (*Pickstone v Freemans plc* (1989)[3]).

OCCUPATIONAL PENSION SCHEMES

Two recent cases before the ECJ *Vroege v NCIV Instituut voor Volkshuisvesting BV*[4] and *Fisscher v Voorhuis Hengela BV*[5] brought the issue of Equal Treatment of male and female employees under Occupational Pension Schemes into the spotlight. In the case of *Vroege* the ECJ held that exclusion of part-time workers from Occupational Pension Schemes could amount to indirect sex discrimination where it has a disproportionate affect on workers on one sex in comparison to the other. As the ECJ has included pensions within within the definition of pay such an employee may succeed in a claim under the EPA unless the employer can establish a genuine material factor defence (discussed below).

The question troubling Industrial Tribunals is how far such claims could be back-dated. In *Fisscher* the ECJ held that national legislation should determine the question of retrospective access to Occupational Pension Schemes.

The Occupational Pension Scheme (Equal Access To Membership) Amendment Regulations 1995 were brought into effect in the UK from 31 May 1995. These Regulations apply the time limits under the EPA to claim for pension scheme membership ie claims must be brought within six months of leaving a particular employer and may be back-dated for a maximum of two years from the date of claim. Employers must provide the necessary funding to secure the entitlement to prospective benefits of employees covered by these new Regulations.

CHOICE OF COMPARATOR FOR THE PURPOSES OF MAKING A CLAIM UNDER THE EQUAL PAY ACT

The comparator must be an employee of the opposite sex and someone in the same employment as the claimant. This therefore includes employees employed by the same or an associated employer either at the same

3 [1989] AC 66 (HL).
4 [1994] IRLR 651.
5 [1994] IRLR 662.

establishment or at establishments within Great Britain in which common terms and conditions of employment apply (either generally or for employees for relevant classes). Claimants will be careful in selecting their comparators for the purposes of making a claim and may chose a past employee provided that employee has been a recent employee and been in a contemporaneous employment with the claimant.

As the claimant's case will hinge upon a very detailed comparison with the employee they nominate as a comparator, they will chose this comparator very carefully and may delay naming them until they have enlisted as much information as possible from the employer through the process of further and better particulars and discovery. The Industrial Tribunal cannot substitute another employee whom it believes may be a more appropriate comparator to the one selected.

CHOOSING COUNTERPARTS WHERE MALE AND FEMALE EMPLOYEES ARE EMPLOYED ON THE SAME TERMS DOING THE SAME WORK

The case of *Pickstone v Freemans Plc* (1989)[6] clearly stated that women employees are not precluded from claiming under section 1(2)(c) of the EPA (ie work of an equal value to work carried out by men in the same employment) by the fact that another man in the same employment is carrying out the same work as that woman for the same pay and on the same terms and conditions. As a consequence, the applicant does not have to choose as her comparator the male colleague in the same employment, but rather can choose someone else who carries out work of equal value to herself, but who is on better terms and conditions.

Two recent cases have also considered the phrase 'in the same employment' for the purposes of a claim under the EPA. The Court of Appeal, in its consolidated judgments in *British Coal Corporation v Smith and Others*[7] and *North Yorkshire County Council v Ratcliffe and Others*[8] came to the conclusion that a comparator employed at a different establishment would have to be employed by the same employer, or an associated employer, on the same terms and conditions as apply, or would apply to employees of the comparator's class at the applicant's establishment. The Court of Appeal was of the view that it was easy in the case of *Leverton v Clwyd County Council*[9] to see that the same terms and conditions of employment applied at the two establishments in question as in that particular case they were both governed

---

6 [1989] AC 66.

7 [1994] IRLR 342.

8 [1994] IRLR 342.

9 [1989] 1 All ER 78.

by a single collective agreement. In other words, the terms and conditions of employment applied generally so far as both female and male employees of those establishments were concerned.

In the present cases, the court was called upon to ascertain exactly what was meant by the phrase 'common terms and conditions' and came to the conclusion that the following criterion needed to be satisfied in order to choose a male comparator from a separate establishment:

(a) The comparator and applicant must have the same employer or an associated employer.

(b) The comparator and applicant would have to have 'common' terms and conditions of employment for men of the relevant class at her establishment ('common' meaning the same as) those of men of the relevant class employed at the women's establishment, or which would be available for male employees for that work at her establishment. The Court of Appeal was of the view that this meant that the terms and conditions for male employees of the relevant class had to be the same in all respects though there was room for small and insignificant differences.

(c) The comparator who was selected must represent the class or group of employees from which he was selected so far as the relevant terms of his contract of employment were concerned.

On the other hand, it was not necessary for the terms and conditions of employment for the female members of staff to be common or the same at both establishments.

GROUNDS FOR MAKING A CLAIM UNDER THE EQUAL PAY ACT

If the Applicant can establish that the comparator is:

Either carrying out:

(a) (i)   like work;

(ii)   equivalent or equivalently rated work;

(iii) work of equal value; and

(b) that his contract contains a term (or terms) which are more favourable than the applicant's;

then the applicant is in a position to show that she has an arguable case, and the onus lies with the employer to establish a defence to the applicant's claim (discussed below). In other words, the burden of proof shifts from the employee to the employer.

DEFENCES TO A CLAIM MADE UNDER THE EQUAL PAY ACT

The genuine material factor defence

This defence applies to all three heads of claim, like work, work rated as equivalent, and work of equal value. To establish this defence under section 1(3) of the EPA the employer must prove beyond reasonable doubt:

(a) that there is a genuine material factor (other than sex discrimination) giving rise to the variation in the complainant's contract from that of the comparator;

(b) that the variation complained of, be it pay, holidays or other contractual terms, is genuinely attributable to the material factor; and

(c) that the material factor giving rise to the variation is not a result of sex discrimination, whether direct, indirect, covert or overt.

To determine whether or not the material factor relied upon by the employer is free from sex discrimination, the Scottish EAT in *Barber v NCR (Manufacturing) Limited* (1993)[10] directed that an Industrial Tribunal in ascertaining what the material factor defence is, should bear in mind that there may still be another cause for the variation complained of which is not a material factor and must therefore ask itself whether that cause (as opposed to the variation) is due to sex discrimination. Industrial Tribunals will therefore consider very carefully the genuine reasons for any variation between a complainant and a comparators' contract of employment and will go behind the causes for the material factor defence put forward by an employer.

Some examples of materials factor defences that have successfully been argued by employers include:

• Different geographical location of the work.

• Higher qualifications which are directly relevant to the job employees are employed to perform.

• Number of hours worked provided that the hourly rate is the same (there is established case law that it is inappropriate to distinguish between part-time and full-time employees by paying a higher hourly rate to full-timers).

• Paying premium rates in a shift cycle to those working anti-social hours.

• Personal circumstances (red circling, eg to preserve an employee's salary whose job was made redundant but who was offered a lower grade job but allowed to retain his salary).

---

[10] [1993] IRLR 95.

- Productivity/performance related pay provided it can be objectively justified on a basis which is free from sex discrimination. The difficulty with this as a material factor is the inevitable subjective element of the assessment of employees performance by different managers. The degree of subjectivity is amplified by the use of subjective assessment criteria such as aptitude and where there is more than one aptitude criteria a significant risk of double counting arises due to overlapping of similar heads of assessment.

- Market forces where, in order to attract candidates of a suitable calibre an employer has found it necessary to increase the rate of pay for new employees but the employers must be careful to constantly monitor such criteria as once the original need has passed, market forces will no longer provide a defence.

- Financial crisis where the financial circumstances of the employer have changed significantly such that the employer cannot afford to pay all of its employees employed in the same or similar work at the same rate. However, as with market forces employers must carefully monitor such criteria as a change in fortunes will mean this defence can no longer be justified.

PAY STRUCTURES DEVELOPED THROUGH COLLECTIVE BARGAINING

Very often in the health service, the level of pay and other terms and conditions of employee's contracts of employment are a result of negotiations between health authorities and the unions. Unfortunately, the ECJ has stated quite categorically that it is up to the employer to show that the difference in pay is based on objectively justified factors unrelated to any discrimination on grounds of sex. The fact that rates of pay were arrived at by separate collective bargaining processes notwithstanding that no discrimination was involved within those processes, was not a sufficiently objective justification for the difference in pay. This can be seen by the case of *Enderby v Frenchay Health Authority* (1993).[11] In that particular case, collective bargaining agreements were in force and as a consequence of those agreements, distinct pay structures were agreed for speech therapists, pharmacists and clinical psychologists. Speech therapists which were/are a predominantly female profession were the lowest paid and the applicant, a speech therapist employed by the health authority, brought proceedings on the ground that

---

[11] [1993] IRLR 591.

she was employed on work of equal value within the meaning of the EPA and was therefore discriminated against on the grounds of her sex. As mentioned above, the fact that the agreement had been negotiated by the trade unions was irrelevant and it was held that it would not justify a difference in pay as the work was for equal value.

MATERIAL FACTOR – PARTIAL DEFENCE

According to the ECJ in *Enderby* mentioned above, if the national court is in a position to determine exactly what proportion of the increase in pay is attributable to the material factor, then it must come to the conclusion that the pay differential is thereby objectively justified to the extent of that particular proportion. On the other hand, if the tribunal cannot determine the proportion, then it must assess on the basis of the evidence before it whether the material factor that is relied upon was sufficiently significant to provide an objective justification for part or all the difference.

FURTHER DEFENCES IN EQUAL VALUE CASES

There are two further lines of defence to an employer in respect of cases based on claims of equal value;

(a) if the Industrial Tribunal is satisfied that there are no reasonable grounds for determining that the work is of equal value; or

(b) where the work of the claimant and the comparator has been the subject of an independent job evaluation study that has not rated it as equivalent and that job evaluation study was itself not discriminatory.

Therefore, employers may argue that there are no reasonable grounds for determining that the Applicant's work is of equal value. In support of such submission the employer may give evidence of an analytical job evaluation study comparing the work of the applicant and her comparator which shows that on an objective analysis the two positions have achieved different ratings under the study. Further, that there are no reasonable grounds for determining that the evaluation in the study was made on a system which discriminates on grounds of sex. Industrial Tribunals determining equal value cases are currently required to order a report to be prepared by an independent expert unless the employer has successfully argued the no reasonable grounds defence. However, the Government has issued a green paper on options for reform for 'Resolving Employment Rights Disputes' which proposes that the use of independent experts in such cases be at the Industrial Tribunal's discretion. Responses to the green paper were submitted by 10 March 1995, at the time of printing Ministers were considering these responses and no further information regarding implementation of the proposals was available.

DETERMINING WHETHER THE WORK OF THE CLAIMANT AND THE COMPARATOR IS OF EQUAL VALUE

For equal value claims and claims of work rated as equivalent where there is no job evaluation scheme the Industrial Tribunal will refer the claim for assessment by an independent expert. This expert is appointed by the Industrial Tribunal to carry out an objective comparative study between the work of the complainant and that of the comparator. Such an assessment is carried out under various criteria, the main ones of which are: the skill, knowledge and experience of the claimant and comparator, their respective levels of responsibility, effort (physical and mental), and working conditions. The independent expert requires the co-operation of both parties in carrying out the assessment and it is quite common for parties to appoint their own experts to liaise on their behalf and prepare their written submissions to the independent expert regarding the jobs that are the subject of the comparison and any relevant matters that the parties may wish to put forward in arguing as to the respective job's value. It is not the independent expert's role to determine whether there is a genuine material factor defence justifying any difference in pay or contractual terms in jobs that may be rated as equal. This is a matter to be determined by the Industrial Tribunal when the hearing is resumed.

DESIGNING CONTRACTS OF EMPLOYMENT TO MEET EMPLOYEES' SPECIFIC NEEDS

Employers must be careful to avoid providing a potential applicant with a contractual term that is less favourable than a comparator, that may result in a claim being made.

The case of *Hayward* mentioned above shows that the correct approach is not to consider the contract as a whole, and determine whether the contract is more or less favourable than the comparators when taking into account all its different terms, but rather that each contractual term should be considered separately and compared on an individual basis with a similar provision in the comparator's contract.

In other words, just because a female employee receives better sickness benefits, for instance, but a lower basic rate of pay, notwithstanding that the two provisions may balance each other out (or indeed that she may come out ahead), all terms and conditions contained within the contract of employment need to be looked at on an individual basis, and the fact that she receives higher benefits is irrelevant to the fact that she receives a lower basic rate of pay. Accordingly, she could bring a claim under the EPA citing the difference in the basic rates of pay.

TIME LIMITS FOR MAKING A CLAIM

There appears to be some confusion on this point, but it would appear that generally speaking, a claim can only be brought by an applicant who has been in employment with the relevant employer within six months preceding the date of the reference (EPA section 2(4)).

Notwithstanding this, it was held in *British Railways Board v Paul* (1988)[12] that this time limit only applied to complaints referred by the Secretary of State and not to ordinary complaints made by individuals (under section 2(1) of the EPA). However, this line of reasoning was not adopted in the Scottish EAT case of *Etherson v Strathclyde Regional Council* (1992)[13] which held that the six month time limit applied to claims presented by individuals as well as those references made by the Secretary of State. Most commentators feel that the latter approach is the correct one and whilst it is certainly possible for an employer to argue (where relevant) that the employee in question left his employment outside of this period, whether or not this argument would succeed is far from certain.

According to the case of *British Railways Board v Paul*, even if equality of pay has been achieved at the date of the individual's application, a claim can still be brought in respect of past inequality in pay at any time during the preceding two years (and possibly longer if the case of *Marshall* is followed).

COST TO THE EMPLOYER OF LOSING A CLAIM

Section 2(5) of the EPA provides that an Applicant is entitled to receive back pay equivalent to the difference in pay between the Applicant and the comparator for up to two years before the date when proceedings were initiated. However, it may well be possible to challenge this two year limit on recovery (which incidentally finds no counterpart in Article 119) by reliance upon the unqualified EU right. In particular, the case of *Marshall v Southampton and South West Hampshire Area Health Authority (2)* (1993) might very well mean that there is an argument that such a limitation is incompatible with the Equal Pay Directive, and as such, should be ignored by

---

[12] [1988] IRLR 20.
[13] [1992] ICR 579.

our Courts and Tribunals. Certainly, an employee would be well advised to make a claim beyond the two year period. By way of background, it was because of the Marshall case, that the Government has removed the limitation that may be awarded in sex discrimination cases, and interest is now available on such awards under the Sex Discrimination and Equal Pay (Remedies) Regulations 1993.

NO CONTRACTING OUT OF THE EQUAL PAY ACT PROVISIONS

A term in a contract that attempts to exclude or limit any provision of the EPA is unenforceable by any person in whose favour the term would operate (see Sex Discrimination Act 1975 section 77(3)). Notwithstanding this, there are two ways in which to ensure that an attempt to settle a complaint brought under the EPA can be enforced. These are as follows:

(a) A Contract (COT 3) settling a complaint to an Industrial Tribunal will be upheld if it was made with the assistance of a Conciliation Officer.

(b) If the qualifying conditions for a Compromise Agreement are met, then such an agreement will also be upheld. In other words, the employee must have received independent, legal advice from a qualified lawyer as to the consequences of her entering into such an agreement.

PROACTIVE CLAIM PREVENTION BY THE EMPLOYER

One way to anticipate a possible claim is to conduct an equal pay audit of the overall pay system in an organisation. Such an audit should illuminate the extent and vulnerability of a particular organisation to equal pay claims and provide a foundation for taking action to resolve those vulnerabilities. In principle, an equal pay audit would analyse and compare pay in all its forms between men and women and also possibly between ethnic groups in order to test whether pay systems are objectively justifiable.

The alternative to a full equal pay audit is to look out for warning signs of potential vulnerability. For example, attention should be paid to the following:

(a) unobjective pay and grade determinations eg where such responsibility rests with line managers;

(b) red circling in perpetuity;

(c) where there is marked gender segregation because of job type, then it may well be that there is gender based pay discrimination. So far as the health service is concerned, this would obviously apply to nurses and special therapists;

(d) lack of central control and monitoring of pay;

(e) bonus or performance related schemes which exclude certain job categories.

Whilst any of the above are not necessarily indicative that an equal pay claim will succeed, they do point to a vulnerability in a particular organisation and if they exist, it is recommended that steps should be taken to rectify the situation.

Employers may also consider conducting a job evaluation study across the organisation or between particular jobs or categories of employees that may be used to defend an equal value claim as discussed above. However, the results of such a study may reveal discrepancies in pay between jobs of equal value that would undermine the employers existing pay structure and require that the pay structure be reviewed.

The other main advantage of preventing a claim is that the employer is then in a position to set his own pay systems without the danger of an Industrial Tribunal imposing a new pay system that has the effect of undermining existing pay structures. The major difficulty is that it may expose vulnerabilities that the employer would rather remained hidden away and that he may either have to deal with or effectively assume the risks for failing to take any action. This was clearly demonstrated in a line of recent cases culminating with *Enderby* where, over a period of years pay structure for different health professionals had evolved through profession specific collective bargaining producing the disparity between female dominated and male dominated professions. The ECJ rejected the collective bargaining defence, although it accepted that the process was not tainted by sex discrimination. As a result the health authority may be forced to eliminate the discrepancies that have developed in its pay structure and harmonise terms and conditions across professional specialisms. Following the ECJs ruling on the preliminary questions, the case has reverted to the UK Courts to determine Dr Enderby's claim for equal pay.

CHAPTER 6

MARKET TESTING – THE ACQUIRED RIGHTS DIRECTIVE 77/187 AND THE TRANSFER OF UNDERTAKINGS (PROTECTION OF EMPLOYMENT) REGULATIONS 1981

THE DIRECTIVE AND TUPE

The Acquired Rights Directive 77/187 (the 'Directive') was introduced in order to protect employees in the event that the business in which they work is transferred. Whereas employees of a company are protected when the company is sold (since the identity of the employer does not change) the employees of an unincorporated business were not and an asset sale could be undertaken instead of a share sale, in order to divest employees of their employment protection rights. Hence the Directive, which sought (largely) to place employees in the same position whether an asset or share sale was taking place.

The Transfer of Undertakings (Protection of Employment) Regulations 1981 ('TUPE') were introduced to implement the Acquired Rights Directive 77/187 (the 'Directive') in the UK. They have a two-fold aim:

- When an employer proposes to transfer his business or part of it to another, both employers should inform or consult with recognised trade unions concerning that proposal.

- As and when the transfer takes place, the contracts of employment of the relevant employees transfer automatically to the new employer.

THE IMPORTANCE OF THE DIRECTIVE AND TUPE TO THE HEALTH SECTOR

The Directive and TUPE are of importance to the health sector, particularly in the market testing of health or ancillary services where such market testing involves a change of provider. Any person in the business of inviting or submitting tenders to perform a service ought to know in advance where they stand in law – how their activities will be interpreted in law. Trade unions also need to know where they stand. This is particularly true, however, of employers and trade unions in the health sector; indeed, there have been a number of important contracting-out cases which focus specifically on health sector activities.

THE IMPORTANCE OF THE DIRECTIVE

There are several reasons why it is important to be familiar with the Directive:

- The Directive is 'directly enforceable' against public bodies in the UK, such as health sector employers. This means that health sector employees can rely directly on provisions of the Directive rather than TUPE; this may be advantageous to them as in certain circumstances the protection offered by the Directive is more extensive.

- As TUPE has emanated from the Directive, developments in the application of the Directive impinge directly upon the way in which TUPE is interpreted by UK courts. Our courts are in fact required to interpret TUPE in every way possible (without actually distorting the words) in order to give effect to the Directive. In other words, they are required to give a 'purposive interpretation' of TUPE.

- European case law which interprets the applicability of the Directive is, therefore, of double relevance to health sector bodies: in interpreting the Directive and in interpreting TUPE to give effect to the Directive. Note, however, that in determining questions referred to it upon the Directive, the European Court does not rule whether or not the Directive will apply to a set of facts, only that the Directive may apply. The Court invariably then goes on to say that it is for the national courts to apply the guidance that it provides to determine whether there indeed has been a transfer.

THE ESSENTIAL FEATURES OF THE DIRECTIVE AND TUPE AS FAR AS THE HEALTH SECTOR IS CONCERNED

Broadly, the key areas are:

- that they apply to any transfer from one person to another of an undertaking, business (or part) in the UK (Article 4(1)/Regulation 3(1));

- that a transfer does not terminate any relevant contract of employment; instead, the contract is deemed to operate after the transfer as if it were originally made between the person employed and the transferee (Article 3(1)/Regulation 5(1));

- if at the time of a transfer, the transferor has a collective agreement with a recognised Trade Union, that collective agreement is protected (Article 3(2)/Regulation 6);

- rights under occupational pension schemes are not transferred (Article 3(3)/Regulation 7);

- if before or after a relevant transfer any employee of the transferor or transferee is dismissed, that dismissal may be automatically unfair (Article 4(1)/Regulation 8(1));

- where, however, any such dismissal can be shown to be for an economic, technical or organisational reason entailing a change in the workforce, the dismissal will not be automatically unfair, but the person dismissing will still have to show that the dismissal was fair within the meaning of section 57(3) of the Employment Protection (Consolidation) Act 1978 (Article 4(1)/Regulation 8(2));

- the recognition of relevant trade unions is transferred (Article 5/Regulation 9);

- both transferor and transferee have duties to inform and consult (with a view to seeking agreement) relevant trade unions; the unions can complain to the Industrial Tribunal if these obligations are not fulfilled (Article 6/Regs 10-11).

Note that the Directive is in the process of being completely revised; the new Directive when in force, will almost certainly stimulate consequential amendments to TUPE. The draft Directive is discussed later in this chapter.

The current provisions are however now discussed in further detail.

THE TRANSFER OF AN 'UNDERTAKING'

The Directive and TUPE broadly apply wherever there is a transfer of an undertaking or business (or part) from one employer to another. The questions to be determined, therefore, are:

- what is an 'undertaking' or 'part an undertaking'? and

- is that undertaking or part 'transferred'?

Originally, TUPE applied only to undertakings that were a trade or business in the nature of a commercial venture. The European Court of Justice ruled, however, that this was too restrictive an interpretation of the Directive, and TUPE was accordingly amended by the Trade Union Reform and Employment Rights Act 1993. Recently, the scope of TUPE has been considerably expanded by the courts. Among the examples of activities which the European Court of Justice has decided may be caught are:

- a foundation providing assistance to drug addicts and funded by grants from a local authority (see *Dr Sophie Redmond Stitching v Bartol* (1992)[1]);

- a canteen service made available by a Company to its employees (see *Rask v ISS Kantineservice A/S* (1993)[2]);

- the cleaning of a bank (see *Christel Schmidt* Case (1994)[3]);

The UK courts have drawn upon the guidance of the ECJ contained in these decisions by ruling that various UK activities amount to undertakings capable of being transferred:

- the provision of paediatric and neonatal in- and out-patient services at an NHS trust hospital (see *Porter and Nanayakkara v Queens Medical Centre (Nottingham University Hospital)* (1993)[4]);

- the cleaning of a health authority hospital (see *Dines & Others v Initial Health Care Services Ltd and Pall Mall Services Group Ltd*[5]).

- management and air traffic control functions (see *Council of the Isles of Scilly v Brintel Helicopters Limited and Others* (1995)[6]).

Looking at these examples, three things become clear. The first is that where the activity in question forms part of the main purposes of the undertaking, the courts, led by the ECJ (see *Redmond*, pp 371-372) have decided that activities without a commercial purpose can be caught. Secondly, the courts have had no difficulty in finding that an activity can constitute 'part' of an undertaking notwithstanding that that activity is entirely ancillary to its main purpose. The cleaning of a hospital, for example, has been found to be a 'separate economic entity' of a health authority's undertaking because it was a self-contained service carried out by contractors with no other obligations to the hospital (see *Dines*[7]). Thirdly, an economic entity can exist even though it comprises only activities and employees or the provision of services (see *Isles of Scilly*).

This line of thinking has been taken to extremes by the ECJ which has decided that a cleaning operation carried on by a bank and performed by just one cleaner constituted 'part' of the bank's undertaking (see *Schmidt*). The court's reasoning was that the existence of a sole employee does not preclude there being a transfer as long as it can be shown that the activity in question constitutes an economic unit with a minimum level of 'organisational independence' which can exist by itself or constitute part of a larger

---

[1]   [1992] IRLR 366.
[2]   [1993] IRLR 133.
[3]   C-392/92 [1994] IRLR 302.
[4]   [1993] IRLR 486.
[5]   [1994] IRLR 336.
[6]   [1995] IRLR 6.
[7]   [1993] IRLR 521 paragraph 9.

undertaking (see *Schmidt*). Given that there now appears to be no limit in size upon what can be transferred, it appears that there may be few, if any, limits on what could be caught. There are indications, however, that the courts may move away from this extreme position (see below).

In considering whether any activity in question is capable of being transferred, either as an undertaking or part of one, we suggest that you review the following 'shopping list' of factors:

- Does the activity constitute a 'stand-alone' service offering particular skills?

- Could the activity be described as 'distinct', 'readily identifiable' or having 'organisational independence' because, for example, it:

  (a) occupies separate premises;

  (b) uses its own equipment;

  (c) has a separate culture;

  (d) operates under its own name or logo;

  (e) has dedicated staff who are not employed to (and do not) work in any other activity in the undertaking;

  (f) requires staff to wear a distinct uniform;

  (g) has separate/dedicated management;

  (h) has a separate profit centre or accounting arrangements?

Is the activity likely to be put out to tender? If it is, it is likely that it does constitute a sufficiently distinct service. The same applies to a service which having been put out to tender, is brought back in-house (see *Isles of Scilly*).

CONCLUSION

Whether or not an activity carried on by a health sector employer is an activity capable of being a 'part' of that provider's 'undertaking' will clearly depend on all the circumstances and it is important to review all aspects of the activity closely. Decided cases will provide a measure of guidance but the question should always be specifically addressed – the answer will not necessarily be a foregone conclusion. It should be borne in mind that the courts may in future retreat from the extreme position adopted in *Schmidt* by insisting on the presence of an 'economic entity' as opposed merely to an 'activity'. It is possible that future amendments to the Directive will prompt the Courts into this course of action. Whether or not this will lead to clarification of whether market testing is caught, however, remains to be seen (see below).

THE 'TRANSFER' OF THE UNDERTAKING

Having decided that there is an undertaking or part capable of transferring, it is then important to establish whether, as a result of the transaction that is envisaged, it will indeed transfer to another. In determining whether this will occur or not, the decisive criterion is whether or not the undertaking 'retains its identity' after the transaction, which will be indicated in particular by the fact that its operation is continued or resumed (see *Rask, Isles of Scilly*).

Whether these conditions are fulfilled is a question of fact and again the following 'shopping list' should be considered:

- What type of undertaking is being transferred?

- Are tangible assets such as buildings or movable property being transferred?

- What is the value of the intangible assets at the time of the transfer?

- Are the majority of the undertaking's employees being taken over by the new employer?

- Are customers being transferred?

- What degree of similarity of activities will there be before and after the transfer?

- What period (if any) of suspension of the undertaking's activities will there be?

It is important to note, however, that all these circumstances are merely single factors in the overall assessment that must be made and cannot be considered in isolation (see *Spijkers v Gebroeders Benedick Abattoir CV*[8]). Note that a transfer may occur notwithstanding that there is no relationship between the current and new providers, no transfer of assets, and no transfer of customers or clients. Furthermore, it matters not that an NHS contract between a health authority or commission and an NHS trust for the provision to the authority by the trust of certain services is not legally enforceable (section 4 National Health Service and Community Care Act 1990); it can still be the subject of a transfer (see *Porter*). Nor will a transfer be prevented by the fact that when a change of provider occurs, overall responsibility for providing that service remains with the Secretary of State, the regional health

---

[8]   [1986] ECR 1119.

authority and district health authority. 'The provider is the person who carries this responsibility [and therefore] ... a change of provider is a change which may bring about a transfer' (see *Porter*, see also *Isles of Scilly*). The European Court has ruled that in deciding whether there is a transfer technical rules must be avoided and the substance matters more than the form; a realistic and robust view must be taken and all the facts considered.

Notwithstanding that no one factor can be considered in isolation, the degree of similarity of activity performed before and after the transfer has received particular attention in recent cases. Courts have been reluctant to find that changes in the activity preclude the existence of a transfer:

'The fact that a business is carried on in a different way is not conclusive against there being a transfer – new methods, machinery, new types of customer are relevant factors but they do not of themselves prevent there being in reality a transfer of an undertaking' (see *Spijkers v Gebroeders Benedik Abattoir CV*[9]).

Where an activity does not lend itself to the employment of many different techniques (such as hospital cleaning), the court has concluded that no significant dissimilarities could arise to prevent a transfer occurring (see *Dines*). The ECJ has also taken the view based on information known to it, that one factor – the transfer of the financing of a drug rehabilitation unit – was of decisive importance notwithstanding minor changes in the way such a unit would be run in future (see *Redmond*).

This factor is clearly of particular relevance to the health sector because of the way in which medical services are currently evolving. An example is a traditional hospital-based in- and out-patient service with limited community involvement which is replaced (by, for example, being put out to tender) by a new consultant-led service with far more emphasis upon the devolution of care to community-based facilities. The court, in considering just such facts, has decided that there would be a transfer of the service, notwithstanding such changes:

'Medical science does not stand still. As it advances, methods of giving. ... care are naturally modified and improved. This process is going on all the time. It does not mean that the object of the undertaking is changing but only that new means of achieving it are being adopted ... We are ... dealing with a type of undertaking in which it is particularly likely that different ways of carrying on the undertaking may be adopted without destroying its identity' (see *Porter*).

That is to say, as long as the activity's character remains essentially the same, a transfer may occur.

This issue should never be treated as a foregone conclusion, however. The courts are willing to find that there has been no resumption of the activity in

---

[9]   [1986] 2 CMLR 486.

cases where changes have been so fundamental that the identity of the previous activity has been destroyed. Where, for example, a NHS hospital shop selling mainly newspapers, magazines, confectionery and flowers and making no profit until its last two years of trading was replaced by the branch of a major chain store which stocked a much wider range of goods and was run on commercial lines, the Employment Appeal Tribunal endorsed the Industrial Tribunal's view that the degree of similarity between the activities carried on before and after the alleged transfer was minimal and that a legal transfer had not occurred (see *Mathieson & Another v United News Shops Ltd*[10]).

The extent to which staff are retained has also been considered with reference to a situation where 'more than half' of the employees were employed by the new employer (see *P Bork International A/S v Foreningen af Arbejdsledere i Danmark*[11]). The fact that a third of the employees were not taken on did not of itself prevent a transfer.

Furthermore, it appears that a change of location will not of itself prevent a transfer (see *Porter*, in which the performance of the paediatric and the neonatal service was moved, in part, from the Grantham & Kesteven General Hospital to the Queens Medical Centre at Nottingham University and to various smaller medical centres).

Moreover, TUPE will not be defeated simply because an activity has transferred only to be subsumed, following the transfer, into a much larger undertaking. If the transferred activity is the same immediately after the transfer as it was before the transfer took place, that is sufficient (see *Farmer v Danzas (UK) Ltd*[12]).

The interpretation of what constitutes the transfer of an undertaking is a rapidly changing area and each new case provides further guidance. The *Mathieson* case may, unless it is successfully appealed, represent the first attempt by the higher courts to demarcate the limits of the application of TUPE in contracting out. Further guidance, however, will be instructive as to the circumstances which would preclude a legal transfer.

FUTURE DEVELOPMENTS – A REVISED DIRECTIVE

Amendments to the Directive are currently being considered and it is anticipated that a completely revised Directive may be implemented by the end of 1996.

The European Commission has been heavily lobbied by business organisations and trade unions in relation to how far, if at all, the new

---

[10] EAT 25 January 1995 (9554/94).

[11] [1989] IRLR 41.

[12] EAT 6 October 1994 (858/93).

Directive should apply to the contracting out and market testing of activities. The draft Directive states, at Article 1, that:

> 'the transfer of an activity which is accompanied by the transfer of an economic entity which retains its identify shall be deemed to be a transfer within the meaning of this Directive. The transfer of only an activity of an undertaking, business or part of a business, whether or not it was previously carried out directly, does not in itself constitute a transfer within the meaning of the Directive.'

It appears then, that the European Commission is unwilling, despite the lobbying, to declare once and for all whether market testing is or is not caught by the Directive. In its explanatory memorandum accompanying the draft Directive, however, the European Commission states that in the absence of explicit Community provisions on this specific point, the European Court of Justice has 'continued its dynamic interpretation activities in a field which is becoming increasingly complex'. It appears, then, that the Commission has declined to provide the clarification that is so urgently sought and that it considers such clarification should and will in due course be provided by the European Court. The Commission does, however, go on to stress the importance of the 'shopping list' of factors set out above. Significantly, it does not place a seal of approval upon the extreme position of the European Court in *Schmidt*.

CONCLUSION

Whether or not an undertaking or part will 'transfer' will, again, depend on all the circumstances. As with the question of what constitutes an undertaking or part, the European Court's decision in *Schmidt* represents the most extreme position. This is that it is enough to show simply that an activity has retained its identity after the transfer; the Court did not expressly apply the 'shopping list' approach (mentioned above) which it had clearly applied in previous cases. It therefore seems as though, as long as the essential nature of the activity remains the same, virtually all cases of market testing (contracting-out, contracting-in and second round competitive tendering) will, in practice, be covered by TUPE and the Directive. Whether or not the revised Directive will substantially change the situation remains to be seen. The authors consider that the way in which the new Directive is interpreted by the European Court will be more significant than the actual revision of the Directive itself. The revision indicates that in future it will not be sufficient for a Court to determine that there has been a transfer simply because an 'activity' has 'retained its identity' without more. However, the UK Court has already found that the contracting-out of a cleaning service amounted to the transfer of an economic entity (not a mere activity (see *Dines*)). On that basis, it would seem unlikely that the Court would have decided differently even under the revised wording. The authors consider that the applicability of the Directive to contracting-out is well established; how far it will be caught by the new Directive will be clarified in due course by the Courts.

STEPS WHICH MAY BE TAKEN TO CLARIFY THE POSITION BEFORE THE EVENT

Given the prevailing uncertainties, it is obviously preferable if a way can be found to determine the question one way or the other before the event. This may be achieved in a number of ways:

- An employee, who is aware that the identity of his employer may change as a result of market testing and that the employer and/or the putative transferee may not comply with their obligations under the Directive and TUPE, may challenge that non compliance in legal proceedings. The High Court has determined, by means of an expedited hearing of an application under Order 14A of the Rules of the Supreme Court, whether or not employees would transfer along with the supply of certain services in advance of the actual transfer (see *Kenny v South Manchester College*[13]). It has been established that such proceedings can be used to determine this question as long as the essential facts can be established even if all remaining issues of fact are unresolved (see *Porter*).

- If a putative transferor and transferee refuse to acknowledge that the Directive and TUPE apply to a proposed transaction, there is a remote possibility that the union would commence proceedings in the Industrial Tribunal against one or both parties for an award in respect of affected employees to reflect the failure of the Respondent(s) to inform or consult that union in accordance with Regulation 10; the rationale would be that these requirements are not fulfilled unless and until the parties acknowledge that the Directive and TUPE apply. There is a possibility, although no guarantee, that the Industrial Tribunal would then helpfully make a declaration as to whether the Directive and TUPE apply; the Tribunal could, however, simply decide that the parties have in any event satisfied the Directive/TUPE consultation requirements and deem it unnecessary to rule upon whether the Directive/TUPE actually apply.

- It may also be possible for an employee in this situation to apply for a declaration from an Industrial Tribunal, in advance of the transfer, that the Directive and TUPE will transfer the employee's contract of employment and that the old employer and new employer have already breached their obligations by failing to inform and consult with the employee's

---

13 [1993] IRLR 265.

representatives. This is as yet an untested area of law, however, and employees pursuing this route will, if successful, risk having to defend an appeal in the Employment Appeal Tribunal or higher courts. It seems unlikely that in fact an employee would be permitted to make such a claim, since the obligation to inform and consult is due only to 'workers representatives' not to employees themselves. Furthermore, an employee may as a precondition have to show he had suffered loss and this may be difficult. It would, however, be a much cheaper course of action for an employee than to file an Order 14A application.

• The obvious practical course of action prior to the event is for all parties – the employer, the putative transferee and the unions – to agree in advance that the Directive and TUPE apply and to proceed accordingly. If the employer and the putative transferee disagree, the matter may be resolved by the taking of indemnities: the party which contends that the Directive and TUPE will not apply ought to be ready to indemnify the party which contend that they do. Note that when the new Directive comes into effect it may be necessary for the transferor to seek an indemnity against any liabilities which he may retain post-transfer (see further below). It is always important, of course, to remember that an indemnity is only as good as the giver. Furthermore, in some cases such as second round competitive tendering and rival bids by NHS trusts to a Health Commission, there may be no incentive for transferor and transferee to co-operate in this way.

IDENTIFYING WHICH EMPLOYEES WILL TRANSFER

Occasionally, difficult questions will arise as to exactly which employees of the old employer (if any) will transfer. If the entity to be transferred is serviced by employees who are 'assigned to' that undertaking, those employees will transfer (see *Botzen v Rolterdamsche Droogdok Maatschpappj BV*[14]). However, whether certain employees are in fact 'assigned to' the undertaking may be in doubt. An employer who has employees involved in the undertaking but who are not 'assigned to' it may be faced with having to declare redundancies as a result of the transfer (and bearing the cost).

The question arising out of the *Botzen* case is what 'assigned to' means. The wider view is that an employee is assigned to a post if, as a matter of practice, he spends most of his time working in relation to that post. There is however a narrower view which states that if an employee's contract makes clear that he can be required to work in various parts of his employer's

---

[14] [1986] 2 CMLR 50.

business and not merely one post, that he is not 'assigned to' any particular post. The courts appear to prefer the narrower view, deciding in one case that a trainee nurse was not 'assigned to' his hospital despite the fact that he had worked there for nine months before a transfer and for a year thereafter. He worked under a training contract under which he could be moved to any other hospital at the direction of the District Health Authority and was not therefore 'part of the human stock' of the hospital concerned (see *Gale v Northern General Hospital NHS Trust*[15]). It appears from this case that merely because an employee works, at the time of transfer, in the part of the undertaking transferred, this will not necessarily guarantee that that employee will transfer. Indeed, if his contract of employment contains the equivalent of a mobility clause, this may indicate that he is not in fact assigned to a particular part of the business and will not necessarily transfer with any part of the business which is then transferred. Only employees who, in practice and under the terms of their contract, work in a particular post that is to be transferred will definitely be 'assigned to' the part of the business to be transferred.

The question of whether an employee is assigned to the undertaking or part which is transferring can be particularly difficult to determine in circumstances where an employee has a group function, and the EAT has given conflicting decisions on the point. On the one hand, the chief executive of a holding company whose role encompassed all of the companies in the group was found not to be employed by any of the four subsidiaries which were transferred (see *Michael Peters Ltd v Farnfield & Another*[16]). In contrast, the EAT in Scotland have ruled that a company secretary with a group function was assigned to a part of the group's undertaking which transferred because he worked very substantially in connection with that part (see *Sunley Turriff Holdings Ltd v Thomson & Others*[17]). Future decisions may resolve the conflict between these cases which, in any event, illustrate that the question of to which part of an undertaking an employee is assigned is the main issue to be resolved.

Note also that only employees of the transferor will transfer. Any individuals who work on secondment in the part of the undertaking being transferred will not transfer but will remain with the transferor.

---

15   [1994] IRLR 292.
16   [1995] IRLR 190.
17   [1995] IRLR 184.

EMPLOYEES WHO TRANSFER FROM A REGIONAL OR DISTRICT HEALTH AUTHORITY TO AN NHS TRUST

These employees would not, strictly speaking, transfer under the Directive/TUPE but under the provisions of the National Health Service and Community Care Act 1990 (see *Gale*). Section 6 of the 1990 Act operates to transfer contracts of employment for certain specified employees, namely:

- anyone who, immediately before the trust's operational date, is employed by a health authority to work solely at, or for the purposes of, a hospital or other establishment or facility which is to become the responsibility of the trust;

- anyone who is employed by a health authority to work at, or for the purposes of, the establishment which is to become the Trust's responsibility and who is covered by a scheme made by the health authority which designates certain people to be covered by section 6; and

- anyone who is employed by the health authority to work at, or for the purposes of, the establishment which is to become the trust's responsibility whether or not solely there and who takes up an offer of employment by the trust made on or after the date of the order establishing the trust but before its operational date.

The legislation would appear to be catch-all but some health authority employees could fall outside the protection which section 6 gives. The Courts have, for example, decided that a student nurse who was employed by a health authority to work at a number of different hospitals and who consequently took up permanent employment with the NHS trust which had in the meantime taken over the hospital at which he had lately been working had continuity of employment only from the commencement of his permanent post with the trust (see *Gale*). Note however that the Court's decision might have been different if the health authority in that case stipulated that the student nurse would be based at the hospital in question but that it would simply have the right to require him to work elsewhere.

THE CONSEQUENCES IF THE DIRECTIVE AND TUPE DO APPLY

There are two main consequences:

- an obligation to inform and consult with representatives of affected employees;

- the automatic transfer of the employer's obligations under the affected employees' contracts of employment to the transferee.

It is vital that any person who is intending to submit a tender ensures that they know what obligations they will undertake if their tender is accepted. Detailed information as to the contract specification, the contracts of employment, the number of employees and all circumstances relevant to the transaction should be set out in the tender documentation. However, a tenderer should not assume that the information in the documentation is complete and correct and should, if possible, raise any queries he has with the putative transferor before submitting the tender. An outside tenderer is obviously in a more difficult position than the in-house bidder since they obviously have limited access to this information. Nevertheless, it is vital that tenderers carry out as full a due diligence exercise as possible. A body inviting tenders should realise that it is in the interests of all parties that maximum information is available to tenderers, subject to that body's need to keep confidential information that could prove useful to competitors.

A body that invites tenders as part of the compulsory contracting-out regime will have special obligations regarding the disclosure of information. These obligations are set out from time to time in Government circulars; at the time of writing the current circulars are in the process of amendment. The authors do not propose in this book to discuss those special obligations in detail.

THE OBLIGATION TO INFORM AND CONSULT

To whom the obligations are owed

Article 6 of the Directive states that the transferor and the transferee owe duties of information (and possibly consultation) to 'the representatives of their respective employees affected by a transfer'.

The representatives in question have until recently been construed in the UK to be recognised trade unions only. Where no Trade Union is recognised, therefore, the practice has been effectively to ignore this obligation. However, on 8 June 1994 the European Court held that the UK could not avoid these duties in this way (see *Commission of the European Communities v United Kingdom of Great Britain Northern Ireland* (1994)[18]) and the UK will introduce legislation to deal with the point. On 5 April 1995, in answer to a Parliamentary question, the Government announced that a consultation document had been produced upon the subject of the new legislation and that views were currently being sought upon it. The main proposals are:

- Employers will be required to consult either with independent recognised trade unions or an elected representative of affected employees. The

---

[18]   [1994] IRLR 392.

employer will be able to choose with which body to consult. If an
employer consults with elected representatives, they will have a defence to
any claim brought by the recognised trade union for failure to consult and
vice versa.

- Legislation will not specify the means by which representatives should be
  elected; that will be left for the employer to agree with the employees. Nor
  is it intended that there should be any restriction on who can be elected;
  the representatives do not have to be employees and may be trade union
  representatives.

- An employer will not have to ensure that there are standing arrangements
  in relation to elected representatives; ad hoc arrangements will be
  acceptable.

- Elected representatives would have the same rights as a trade union
  representative; for example, the right not to be unfairly dismissed as a
  result of being a representative.

- It is proposed that rather than consulting 'at the earliest opportunity'
  employers be required to consult 'in good time'.

- Elected representatives would have the right to complain of a failure to
  consult.

The substitution of the words 'in good time' for the present 'at the earliest
opportunity' evidences the Government's intention to comply with the
Directive. However, there is no explanation as to how the two phrases differ
and 'in good time' will inevitably be interpreted by case law in the future. The
draft legislation is expected to be laid before Parliament before the 1995
summer recess but to become law only in autumn 1995.

By whom the obligations are owed

The duty to inform and consult is owed by the transferor and transferee. In
circumstances where, for example, a health authority contracts out a service to
an NHS Trust, assuming TUPE applies, the health authority will be the
transferor and the NHS Trust the transferee. In a second generation round of
tendering, however, where, say, the contract to perform the service is lost by
the first NHS Trust and passes to another, it might be thought that the duty to
inform and consult falls only upon the Trusts and not the health authority.
However, the health authority will also have a duty to inform and consult in
these circumstances. The reasoning is that the health authority, being the
instigator of the process by which the contract passes to another Trust with
possible ramification for affected employees, ought to be part of the
information and consultation process; the legal rationale is that because the
contract momentarily passes back to the health authority before being put out
once more to the second Trust, the health authority momentarily becomes

transferee and then transferor in the process (see *Unison v Leeds City Council (1) and City of Leeds College of Music (2)*[19]).

Information which must be given

The transferor must inform the affected employee's representatives of the following matters:

- the fact that the relevant transfer is to take place;
- when approximately the transfer is to take place;
- the reasons for the transfer;
- the legal, economic and social implications of the transfer for the affected employees;
- the 'measures' which either the transferee or the transferor envisages he will take in connection with the transfer in relation to those employees;
- if the transferee or transferor envisages that he will take no such 'measures', the fact that he will take no such 'measures'.

The meaning of 'measurers' is obscure. It is, however, established that this will include a specific reduction in the level of manpower but not mere possibility or forecasts (see *IPCS v Secretary of State for Defence*[20]). Closure of a ward or the reduction in the number of shifts required would be included; a change of pension rights would not.

The duty to consult

The duty to consult the representatives as opposed to the duty to inform is triggered when either the new or the old employer envisages that he will be taking 'measures' in relation to any of the affected employees. The employer must then consult 'with a view to reaching agreement'. Specifically, an employer, by Regulation 10(6) of TUPE, is obliged to consider any representations made by Trade Union representatives, to reply to those reasons and if they are rejected, to state his reasons.

When to start the process of information (and consultation)

Neither the Directive nor TUPE lay down any rigid timescale. The Directive makes clear that information must be provided and consultations take place 'in good time' before the change in the business is effected (Article 6(3)).

---

[19]   Leeds Industrial Tribunal no 17611/94.

[20]   [1987] IRLR 373.

TUPE, on the other hand, states that the process should begin long enough before the transfer occurs so as to enable consultations (if required) between the transferor and the union representatives to take place. As we explain above, however, the anomaly is due to be irradicated by an amendment to TUPE, expected in the autumn of 1995.

In order to ensure as far as possible that sufficient time is made for such consultations, the transferor should structure his overall transfer timetable in such a way that formal notification to the unions of the required information is made as soon as a definite decision to proceed with the transfer has been taken. Furthermore, enough time should be allowed between the appointment of the contractor and the completion of the transfer itself to allow sensible consultations (if such are required) to take place between the transferee and the union representatives. The transferor should also ensure that he holds talks with the transferee to gauge what plans, if any, the transferee has to take 'measures' so that the transferor can then pass any relevant information in good time to the representatives.

The defence if these obligations are not complied with

Under TUPE (Regulation 10(7)), if there are 'special circumstances which render it not reasonably practicable' for an employer to inform or consult as he is required, the employer is nevertheless obliged to take all such steps towards performing those duties that are reasonably practicable in the circumstances. This derogation has no basis in the Directive and arguably constitutes a breach by the UK of its duty to fully implement the Directive.

However, the transferor arguably has a 'special circumstance' defence if the transferee has breached his duty under Regulation 10(3) to give the transferor such information at such a time as will enable the transferor to perform the duty to inform the union representatives of measures which the transferee envisages he will take in relation to the transfer. The transferor will not, however, be able to argue that there were therefore special circumstances rendering it not reasonably practicable for him to perform that duty unless the transferor gives the transferee notice of his intention to argue that fact before the Industrial Tribunal. By giving the transferee such notice, the transferor joins the transferee in as a party to the proceedings brought by the union. It is suggested that if the transferor is intending to rely on this defence, he should issue his notice to the transferee as soon as possible and preferably as part of the Notice of Appearance. As far as we are aware, there are no cases in which this defence has been successfully invoked.

The 'special circumstances' defence may be revised to take account of the new Directive. It is suggested in the draft Directive that domestic courts should take no account of any defence that an employer could not comply with the information and consultation provisions because the decision which led to the transfer was taken by a head office or controlling body based elsewhere.

The sanction for failing to comply with the duties to inform and consult

An employer who fails to comply with these duties is liable, upon complaint by a trade union to an Industrial Tribunal, to pay an amount in respect of each affected employee which is no greater than four weeks pay for each employee. The Tribunal has a discretion to award up to this maximum 'such compensation as the Tribunal considers just and equitable having regard to the seriousness of the failure of the employer to comply with his duties'. The maximum award is rarely ordered in practice. The courts have emphasised that the Tribunal should weigh the loss suffered by the employees and the seriousness of the employer's conduct in relation to them (see *W Devis & Sons Limited v Atkins*[21]).

A union which is considering making such a complaint must generally do so within three months beginning with the date on which the transfer is completed.

Within three months of the date of the Tribunal's order that the transferor or transferee pay such compensation, an employee may complain to the Tribunal on the grounds that he is an employee of a description to which the order relates and that the transferor or transferee has failed, wholly or in part, to pay him compensation due to him following the order.

THE AUTOMATIC TRANSFER OF THE CONTRACT OF EMPLOYMENT

Assuming that there has been a 'transfer of an undertaking', the rights and obligations of the old employer under the relevant employee's contract of employment will be automatically transferred to the new employer. In effect, the new employer will step into the shoes of the old employer and the contract will be deemed to have been made by the new employer.

This applies to all employees 'employed immediately before the transfer' (Regulation 5(3)). This phrase has been considered by the Court (see *Litster v Forth Dry Dock & Engineering Co Ltd*[22]). The case established the following:

- the time of the transfer means completion;

---

[21] [1977] ICR 662.
[22] [1989] IRLR 161.

- the period 'immediately before' the transfer means the instant before, that is if a person is dismissed even moments before completion, he is not employed immediately before the transfer;

- the principle of automatic transfer cannot be avoided by dismissal effected prior to completion. If TUPE could be avoided in this way, the purpose of the Directive would be defeated.

In practice, the principle established above means that unless the dismissal is for an ETO reason (see below) liability for the dismissal (and the risk of re-instatement) transfer to the transferee.

It seems clear that liability for a dismissal which takes place before a decision is made to contract-out the activity in which the employee was employed would not pass to the transferee. However, query whether such liability would pass if such a decision had already been taken and tenders invited, notwithstanding that at the time of the dismissal the identity of the transferee was not known. Recent case law indicates this lack of knowledge would not of itself prevent that liability transferring (see *Ibex Trading Company Limited v Walton and Others and Alpine (Double Glazing) Company*[23]). These matters will inevitably be addressed by the Courts in future.

As we discuss below, Regulation 8(1) provides that dismissal arising from the transfer will be automatically unfair if the reason or principle reason for the dismissal is the transfer itself.

The obligations and rights transferred

TUPE provides that if the transfer or a reason connected with it is the reason or principle reason for an employee's dismissal that dismissal will be automatically unfair (Regulation 8(1)). Furthermore, if an employee is asserting that his dismissal was in connection with a transfer, he will not have to show, in bringing his claim, that he has two or more years continuous employment (see *Milligan & Another v Securicor Cleaning Ltd*[24]).

The defence available to the employer

However, the employer may have a defence if the employer can establish that an economic, technical or organisational ('ETO') reason entailing changes in the workforce of either the old employer or the new employer before or after the relevant transfer is the reason or principle reason for the dismissal. If so, the dismissal is not automatically unfair and may be a fair dismissal for 'some

---

[23] [1994] IRLR 564 paragraph 25.

[24] EAT/918/94.

other substantial reason' (Regulation 8(2)). The onus of establishing this is on the employer and he must still have acted fairly and equitably in accordance with section 57(3) Employment Protection (Consolidation) Act 1978.

It seems, however, as though an employer will not be able to establish an ETO reason if a dismissal has taken place prior to the transfer and the dismissal was due to the need to cut the overhead costs of the undertaking and, therefore, make it more attractive to the potential new operator purchaser. The ETO defence will only be available if the reason for the dismissal is a reason connected with the conduct of the undertaking. If the dismissal takes place in order to make the undertaking more attractive for sale or some other transfer related reason, that is not a dismissal in connection with the conduct of the undertaking (see *Ibex Trading Co Ltd v Walton*).

Examples of cases in which an ETO reason could be argued are:

- where a need to reduce numbers produces redundancies;
- where a change in organisation brings about changes in job duties;
- where the undertaking is carried out in a different way notwithstanding that the numbers of employees required remains the same (see *Porter* – this indicates that the scope of the ETO defence is a little wider than redundancy (although not perhaps as wide as the 'some other substantial reason' defence under section 57(1)(b) EPCA 1978)).

Dismissals prior to the transfer which are unconnected with the transfer

If a dismissal prior to completion of a transfer is by reason of the transfer and, therefore, in contravention of Regulation 8(1), liability for the dismissal (which is likely to be automatically unfair given the difficulty of making out an ETO reason) will transfer to the new employer. However, if a dismissal prior to completion is for a wholly independent reason – by reason of conduct or capability for example – both the Directive and TUPE make clear that liability will remain with the old employer.

What precisely does transfer

The rights and obligations of the employees' contracts are transferred and continuity of employment is preserved. It should be noted, however, that the following rights and obligations are not transferred:

- the employees' pension rights (the extent of this exclusion has been clarified somewhat but is still far from clear and we consider this further below);
- any criminal liabilities of the previous employer;

- any claim by a trade union that there has been a failure to consult in relation to redundancies.

It has recently been clarified, however, that liabilities in tort, such as negligence claims, can transfer to the new employer even though at the time the actions arose the new employer did not yet exist (see *Wilton & Others v West Cumbria Health Care NHS Trust*[25]). Tort liabilities ought to transfer because Regulation 5(2)(b) of TUPE provides that anything done by the transferor before the transfer in respect of a person employed in the undertaking transferred is deemed to have been done by the transferee. Furthermore, the courts have now accepted that an employer's liability to its employees is based on a 'special relationship' that is a product of both the employment relationship and the contract of employment. A liability for, say, negligence – arising out of the employment relationship – is therefore a liability 'in connection' with the contract of employment and is thus transferred to the new employer along with the rest of the contract.

Pension rights

The Directive expressly provides that a right to 'old age, invalidity or survivors benefits in supplemental or inter-company pension schemes outside the statutory social security schemes in Member States' do not transfer (Article 3(3)). The Directive goes on to provide that 'Member States shall adopt the measures necessary to protect the interests of employees and of persons no longer employed in the transferor's business at the time of the transfer ... in respect of rights conferring on them immediate or prospective entitlement to old age benefits, including survivors' benefits, under supplementary schemes'.

The current interpretation by the UK of this issue is that an occupational pension scheme falls within the exclusion of TUPE and that the new employer will not be obliged to provide a pension to a transferred employee that is no less beneficial than that provided by the old employer. The obligations of the old employer extend merely to protecting the pension rights of employees which have accumulated up to the moment of transfer (see *Waldon Engineering Co Ltd v Warrener*[26]). However, current Government guidance to NHS trusts is that transferees ought to provide equivalent pensions (the Government Actuary will provide a certificate of equivalence). This stems from apparent concern within the Government that since the NHS is a state employer, the UK government may be in breach of Part 2, paragraph 3 of Article 3 of the Directive if it fails to ensure equivalent pension provision.

---

[25] 3.8.94 Newcastle-upon-Tyne County Court.

[26] [1993] IRLR 420.

As yet, there is no judicial interpretation of whether a transferred employee who is deprived of pension rights in respect of future service will have any statutory remedies against either his new or old employer, nor whether such an employee would have a claim for breach of contract against his old employer for failing to ensure that he enjoyed the benefit of equivalent pension arrangements post transfer. The authors consider that an employee would have considerable difficulty in bringing any such claim. However, cases testing the transfer of pension provision are currently waiting to be heard by the courts (*Aindow v (1) Sefton MBC and (2) Brophy Plc* and *Adams v (1) Lancashire County Council and (2) BET Plc*).

Note that the Trade Union Reform and Employment Rights Act 1993 introduced an amendment to TUPE clarifying the fact that if an occupational pension scheme contains any provisions (eg relating to redundancy entitlement) those provisions will be treated as not being part of the scheme. Those benefits would then transfer.

Restrictive covenants

The extent to which a restrictive covenant can be enforced against an employee following a transfer has been an area of considerable doubt. As TUPE operates to transfer all the obligations and rights under the contract of employment to the new employer, does this mean that the restrictive covenant is to be read as a restriction in respect of the new employer or does it continue to operate against the old employer?

The Court of Appeal has now held that a restrictive covenant continues to relate to the business contacts of the original employer and not to those of the new employer (see *Morris Angel & Son Ltd v Hollande & Lee*[27]). The reason for this is that if the covenants were enforceable against the new employer it would turn the obligation under the restrictive covenant into quite a different and possibly much wider obligation than before the transfer. Furthermore, that different obligation was not remotely in the contemplation of the parties when they entered into the agreement containing the covenant and the covenant might therefore place a more restrictive burden on the employee. Accordingly, an employer to whom an employee transfers would be able to enforce the covenant only in so far as the old employer could enforce it. If, for example, an employee transferred with a valid covenant that he would not after the termination of the contract contact the customers of his employer for a certain period, the new employer at the termination of that contract could only prevent the employee from contacting customers of the old employer, not the new employer.

---

[27] [1993] IRLR 169.

Share option/profit share/bonus scheme

The question of whether the transferee should make equivalent provisions in respect of such benefits or, if this is not possible, compensate the employees for loss of such benefits is not at all clear. However, since TUPE transfers duties and liabilities under or in connection with the contract of employment, it could very well be argued that if an individual is entitled to membership of a bonus scheme by virtue of the fact that they are an employee, the obligations of the transferor under the scheme are obligations 'in connection with' the contract of employment and therefore transfer. Clearly, there can be intense difficulties for the transferee in making equivalent provision for the employees but it appears that they would be obliged, at the very least, to take all reasonable steps to compensate the employees for loss of that benefit.

To what extent can the terms and conditions of employment of transferred employees be changed

In general, the new employer has the same rights in respect of changing an employee's terms and conditions of employment as any employer under national law outside the context of a transfer of undertakings, unless the changes are brought about as a result of the transfer (see *Rask*).

Where a change in terms and conditions is not connected with a transfer, the normal rules will apply. That is, that employers cannot unilaterally change terms and conditions of employment without the employee's consent. Where an employer attempts to do so, and the change is fundamental, there is a risk that the contract will be repudiated and that claims of constructive dismissal will arise.

Where a change in terms and conditions is connected with a transfer, the employee receives special protection under Regulation 5(5). This provides that the employee has the right to terminate his contract of employment as a result of substantial changes to the terms and conditions which are to his detriment. It would then be open to the employee to claim that he had been constructively dismissed and such a dismissal would be automatically unfair unless the employer could show an economic, technical or organisational reason entailing a change in the workforce. It is now clear that the ETO defence will apply if the need to protect employees is outweighed by the need for the employer to make economic changes to the business (see *Trafford v Sharpe and Fisher (Building Supplies) Limited*[28]). Note however that the ETO reason must entail a change in the workforce – a change in terms and conditions that is not connected to a need to make changes in the numbers

---

[28] [1994] IRLR 325.

employed will not constitute an ETO reason (see *Berriman v Delabole Slate*[29]). The ETO defence would not, therefore, cover a case where a transferred employee's rate of pay was reduced to bring it into line with existing employees (see, however, further comment *supra*.)

In practice, this means that an employer taking over a business will have to be prepared to continue to meet the obligations formerly met by the old employer – at least for a period. The length of this period is not clear but the Directive indicates that the period should be at least 12 months. Clearly, the longer the period which elapses post transfer, the less likely the employees are to be able to argue that changes in terms and conditions are connected with the transfer.

An employer should also be aware that if transferred employees enjoy terms and conditions more beneficial than those of his existing employees, he may be obliged to improve the terms and conditions of the existing workforce to those of the transferred employees in order to avoid possible equal pay or industrial relations problems.

THE SHARING OF LIABILITY BETWEEN TRANSFEROR AND TRANSFEREE

It seems that liability may in future be shared between transferor and transferee. The situation at present is that liability in respect of contracts of employment and in respect of any dismissal (connected with the transfer) that occurs prior to the transfer, passes to the new employer (see *Ibex Trading*). The transferor can only be held liable for dismissals pre-transfer which have nothing to do with the transfer.

However, when the Directive is revised it seems as though member states will be obliged to introduce legislation which imposes joint liability upon transferor and transferee in respect of liabilities arising out of the contract of employment or employment relationship (although not necessarily pre-transfer dismissal liability). It is also likely that, if this does occur, the UK will take advantage of the proposed limitation upon this principle which is that the transferor will be jointly liable only in respect of such liabilities that arise prior to the transfer and that fall due within the first year after the transfer date.

---

[29] [1985] IRLR 305.

THE RIGHT OF THE EMPLOYEE TO OBJECT TO THE AUTOMATIC TRANSFER OF HIS EMPLOYMENT CONTRACT TO THE TRANSFEREE

As originally drafted, Regulation 5 simply provided for the automatic continuation of the contract of employment between transferee and employee without the consent of either party. However, the European Court has ruled that this is an incorrect interpretation of the Directive; an employee is not prevented from objecting to the transfer and the Directive cannot be construed as obliging an employee to continue his employment relationship with the transferee (see *Katsikas v Konstantinidis*[30]). The European Court has also ruled that it is for member states to decide the fate of the contract of employment or employment relationship with the old employer if the employee refuses to transfer.

The Trade Union Reform and Employment Rights Act 1993 took account of this ruling and Regulation 5 (as amended) now allows an employee who objects to the transfer to assert that objection by informing the transferor or transferee that he objects to becoming employed by the transferee. However, if the employee does object to the transfer, the transfer will operate to terminate the contract of employment with the transferor but the employee will not be treated for any purpose as having been dismissed by the transferor. The employee, therefore, has no employment protection rights or contractual rights following the termination of his contract in this manner.

The UK Courts have taken this point one step further in ruling that TUPE cannot operate to transfer the contract of employment of an employee until that employee has notice both of the fact of transfer and the identity of the transferee. This is because the employee has a right to refuse to be transferred and cannot exercise this right if he does not have this information. The result of this ruling is that an employee who carries on working after the transfer without realising that he is working for a new employer may, if the new employer goes into liquidation, assert his statutory and contractual rights against his old employer (see *Photostatic Copiers (Southern) Ltd v Okuda and Japan Office Equipment Ltd (in liquidation)*[31]).

---

[30] [1993] IRLR 179.
[31] [1995] IRLR 11.

CHAPTER 7

DISMISSAL – SPECIAL FEATURES IN THE HEALTH SERVICE

INTRODUCTION – THE LAW OF UNFAIR DISMISSAL

The law of unfair dismissal is a large and complicated subject and is beyond the scope of this book. The brief principles will however be outlined in this introduction before we turn to look at special features of the health service that have an impact upon dismissals and upon defending unfair dismissal claims. What is known as 'wrongful dismissal' that is to say dismissal in breach of contract, is examined later in this chapter

For unfair dismissal purposes, under section 55(2) of the Employment Protection (Consolidation) Act 1978 a dismissal occurs if:

(a) the employer terminates the employment either on notice or summarily; or

(b) if the employer does not renew a fixed term contract on expiry; or

(c) the employee resigns (whether on notice or not) in circumstances where the employee is entitled to resign because the employer's conduct amounts to a serious breach of contract.

In addition, if a woman has sought to exercise her right to return to work after contractual or statutory extended maternity leave and she is not permitted by the employer to return, this is a deemed dismissal for unfair dismissal purposes (section 56 of the EPCA see Chapter 3).

If an employee has been dismissed then the onus is on the employer to show that the reason for dismissal was one of the 'potentially fair' reasons set out in section 57 of the EPCA. Those reasons are:

(a) the employee's conduct;

(b) the employee's capability or qualifications (this includes ill health);

(c) continued employment would be illegal;

(d) the employee is redundant;

(e) 'some other substantial reason'.

Having established that the reason for dismissal was one of these reasons, the Tribunal then has to determine whether, having regard to all the circumstances of the case (including the size and administrative resources of the employer) the employer has acted reasonably or unreasonably in treating the reason as sufficient for dismissal. In other words, the mere fact that there is a potentially fair reason does mean that the dismissal is fair – perhaps the employer should have waited longer for the sick employee to recover or perhaps the employer should have 'carried' surplus employees until there was a pick up in business rather than have made them redundant.

It is now clear law that in determining whether or not the employer acted fairly the Tribunal should not substitute its own decision on the facts and evidence facing the employer, but should merely assess whether the employer's decision was one that fell within the range of reasonable responses – in other words if some employers would have dismissed in the circumstances and others would not, the employer is entitled to a finding that the dismissal was fair. This principle is set out in the case of *Iceland Frozen Foods Ltd v Jones* (1982).[1] Of course, in practice whether the Tribunal members feel personally that the decision is fair or not will have a significant impact upon their decision, but nevertheless Tribunal hearings can be won by an employer on the basis of the 'range of reasonable responses' even when it is quite clear that all three Tribunal members would have made a different decision.

The question of 'reasonableness' affects both the merits of the decision itself and the way in which the employer went about making the decision, that is to say the procedure adopted by the employer. Quite frequently, the Tribunal will find that the procedure was defective but that if the defect had not occurred, the decision would still have been to dismiss. Indeed, in the real world it is very difficult for there ever to be a dismissal that is procedurally perfect.

A series of cases, starting with the House of Lords case of *Polkey v A E Dayton Service Ltd* (1987),[2] have established that where there are procedural imperfections the possible outcomes are as follows:

- The Tribunal comes to the conclusion that the imperfection was not sufficiently serious to make the decision to dismiss unfair – it is particularly likely to reach such a conclusion if it can be demonstrated that a reasonable employer could decide, or even better that the particular employer concerned did decide, to abridge or shorten the procedure.

- That the defect in procedure made the dismissal unfair but that even if the defect had not occurred the decision would have been the same. In such circumstances the employee is likely to receive the basic award for unfair dismissal but no compensatory award.

- That the defect rendered the procedure unfair and if the procedure had been correct the employee would have been employed for a longer period

---

1   [1982] IRLR 439.
2   [1987] IRLR 503.

whilst that procedure was completed, but would then have been dismissed. In such circumstances the employee is likely to be awarded the basic award plus lost take home pay for the period that it would have taken until the procedure had been exhausted.

- That the defect in the procedure made the decision to dismiss unfair and that there is a chance that had the correct procedure been followed the employee would not have been dismissed. Such a finding will often lead to full compensation although a Tribunal can in theory award a percentage to reflect the chances.

The remedy for unfair dismissal is usually compensation consisting of the basic award and the compensatory award. The basic award is calculated in the same way as the *statutory* redundancy payment. In the health service, continuous service with different health service employers counts as continuous employment for statutory redundancy payment purposes (the Redundancy Payments (National Health Service) (Modification) Order 1993). This Order does not apply to the calculation of the basic award so that a change in health service employer will break continuity unless that change occurred in circumstances to which the Acquired Rights Directive[3] applies – that is to say the employee was transferred from one employer to another together with an undertaking or part of an undertaking.

The compensatory award is to reflect the employee's loss in pay and benefits until he or she finds new work with the same level of pay. In practice Tribunals rarely award more than one year's loss. The compensatory award is limited to £11,000 no matter how great the employee's loss.

Although compensation is the most frequent remedy, in fact the primary remedies for unfair dismissal are reinstatement in the old job together with compensation for earnings lost in the meantime or re-engagement in another job, again together with compensation for earnings lost. An employer can resist an order for re-instatement or re-engagement on the grounds that it is not reasonably practicable, but if the order is nevertheless made and upheld, he can refuse to obey the order. The consequence of such a refusal is extra compensation for the employee.

Certain categories of unfair dismissal carry with them extra, penal, compensation. This applies in particular to dismissals for Trade Union membership or activities, or Trade Union non-membership, and to certain dismissals for health and safety reasons. Any dismissal which also involves sex discrimination or race discrimination will enable the Tribunal to award compensation for loss without the statutory cap of £11,000.

---

[3]　No 77/187/EEC.

HEALTH SERVICE DISMISSAL PROCEDURES

Historically, for most health service employers dismissal procedure were governed by section 40 of the GWC Conditions of Service. In fact, section 40 said little of detail about disciplinary procedures below the appeal stage and most health service employers have created their own well-drafted, detailed procedures which take account of the ACAS Code of Practice. At the appeal stage, section 40 contained more detail. Most NHS Trusts have now negotiated adapted dismissal and appeal procedures with the trade unions involved. Section 40 was replaced in March 1995 by section 42 which gives similar guidance, but less detail on appeals.

Certain categories of staff, in particular doctors and dentists, have the benefit of special procedures under paragraph 190 of the various terms and conditions of service documents applying to them. There are also certain recommended procedures under HC (82)13 and HC (90)9 again applying to medical and dental staff.

RECURRENT PROBLEMS WITH HEALTH SERVICE DISMISSALS

The authors have over the years acted for Health Service employers in connection with many unfair dismissal cases and certain characteristic problem areas have repeatedly demonstrated themselves.

Problem area 1 – lack of management action

Many health service employees have under-performed or misbehaved over long periods without adequate management action having been taken. There are various reasons for this. For example, many private sector employers would suggest that the absence of a profit motive is a significant contributor. Unwieldy procedures, which are dealt with below, have certainly contributed in many cases.

The fact remains that very often employees have performed at a standard below an acceptable one without proper management or disciplinary action having been taken. This then makes it difficult to justify dismissal when a manager eventually does decide to take action. This problem is at its worst in cases where patience finally runs out and the employee is dismissed for conduct or performance of a kind that previously had not even led to a warning.

Any manager who inherits this kind of situation need not despair since action can be taken. The first requirement is to establish clearly what standards are expected and then to work towards those through counselling and, if necessary, warnings. In other words, the fact that an employee has been allowed to under-perform for many years does not mean that he or she then has a right to do so for the rest of their career.

Sometimes managers have not been completely inactive when faced with an under-performing employee but have moved the employee to another department or unit in the hope that things will work out better there. It is not uncommon to come across a case where an employee has been dismissed without previous warning and where, on investigation, it turns out that he or she was dismissed because they had failed, without disciplinary action being taken, in every other department in which he or she could work within the organisation and there was nowhere left for them to go.

Problem area 2 – unwieldy procedures

Procedures are of course vital to ensure consistency, accuracy and fairness. Nevertheless, they can become unrealistic or be used as an excuse for inaction. Most NHS Trusts have given considerable attention recently to simplifying and clarifying lines of management responsibility and there is reason to hope that buck-passing and memo-sending will reduce.

One particular problem with health service dismissals in the past has been that most appeals procedures have involved a dismissed employee having a right to be heard by three members of the health authority which employed them. In many authorities, experience showed that the members were often over-sympathetic and reinstated dismissed employees. The consequence for managers was that after a great deal of effort in gathering information and after two complicated and distressing hearings, the eventual outcome was victory for the employee and a 'slap in the face' for the management side and its witnesses. The advent of NHS Trusts has certainly made a change here with most Trusts ensuring that appeal panels contain at least one executive manager.

Problem area 3 – delay

Because disciplinary action in the health service is normally dealt with carefully and statements are properly prepared and provided to the employee before the disciplinary hearing, some delay is inevitable. Unfortunately, the number of participants at disciplinary and appeal hearings (management side representatives, management side witnesses, the employee, staff side representatives, staff side witnesses, three panel members, clerk or secretary, personnel department representative) means that it often takes many months for a hearing to be arranged. If the hearing cannot be completed in the time allotted, there is then often further delay. It can take a year from the incident occurring to the appeal against dismissal being heard.

Delay does bring the risk of injustice: witnesses' memories fade and witnesses do move away or die. Furthermore, the employer may end up paying a suspended employee for many months whilst getting no work in return. On the other hand, if the employer decides that the employee need not be suspended, the staff side are almost certain to argue that the conduct or poor performance cannot have been that bad and that therefore the employee should not be dismissed.

Problem area 4 – precedents

Unfortunately the lack of management action in some areas can create precedents that unsatisfactory employees can use to their advantage. Employees do from time to time successfully show that their dismissal was unfair because, although their behaviour or performance was unsatisfactory, it was no worse than that of someone else who remains in employment. This is not an insurmountable problem provided that it is spotted and dealt with consciously – the employer should make clear to employees what the new standard is or that the existing standard is now going to be vigorously enforced and then ensure consistency.

Problem area 5 – publicity

A health service employer may be much more sensitive about adverse publicity concerning the workings of any particular unit than a run-of-the-mill employer.

Industrial Tribunal hearings and court trials are public and are often reported in the press. Inevitably, the racier the story, the more likely it is that there will be publicity. Often the publicity will be unwelcome for both employer and employee but in many other cases one party will be much more affected by fear of publicity than another. This is likely to affect that party's willingness to settle the case.

The general principle of open justice is qualified in two respects. First, any court or Industrial Tribunal can take special measures to protect confidential information. Information relating to the health and treatment of patients will usually be heard in private without press or public admitted. Secondly, measures can be taken to protect information, the disclosure of which will cause substantial injury to the undertaking of the employer. Information relating to the finances and business plans of an NHS Trust could fall within this category and may also fall within the confidential information category, and a court or Tribunal should agree to hear that evidence in private if a sufficiently detailed case is made to it to demonstrate the confidentiality of the information and to explain the adverse consequences that would flow from that information being made known publicly. Until the creation of the internal market, an argument that such information was confidential would have carried little weight. Even now, since NHS Trusts are still part of the public service, Tribunals and courts are likely to require a considerable amount of persuasion to treat such information as appropriate for protection by a private hearing.

Special rules have been introduced in the Industrial Tribunals in relation to allegations of sexual harassment or sexual offences (Trade Union Reform and Employment Rights Act 1993). In a case involving sexual misconduct of any kind the Tribunal may make a Restricted Reporting Order preventing any reporting in the written or broadcast media of any information that might identify the people involved in any allegation of sexual misconduct (whether someone making the allegation or someone affected by it). Such a ban will last only until the Tribunal has published its decision whereupon full details can be reported – the theory being that any adverse effect on reputations will at that stage be justified as the Tribunal will have found the allegations either proved or disproved and will have said so in its decision.

The way in which this new discretionary power has been interpreted by Industrial Tribunals is varying from one Tribunal to another and as yet there is no guidance from the Employment Appeal Tribunal or any higher court. Some Tribunals are making restricted reporting orders as a matter of course whereas others are making them only in cases where the allegations involve special features, such as children or particularly outrageous conduct. The better view is probably that a restricted reporting order should be made in most cases, but at the moment the risk of full publicity remains a valid one in sexual harassment cases.

The second special new power of Industrial Tribunals relates to cases that involve an allegation of a criminal sexual offence. In such a case the Tribunal will take steps to delete from the Tribunal paperwork, including the eventual decision, any information that could enable the public to identify the people making or affected by the allegation. This protection is therefore a permanent one.

The combination of these two powers means that in a case involving an allegation of a criminal sexual offence, the Tribunal will probably make a restricted reporting order applying to the hearing itself so that the parties involved cannot be identified in press reports (although the public can still attend to hear the salacious evidence) and the decision itself will not contain the names. Oddly, it does seem that the press could, after the decision has been promulgated, publish the names if they can discover them (for example by attending the hearing).

These new rules have a double effect. First, they make it easier for the victims of sexual harassment to see their cases through and therefore it is more likely that such claims will be made in the first place than was so in the past. Secondly, the new rules also make it easier for employers to take the firm action that they should take against the perpetrators of sexual harassment since adverse publicity is less likely and, particularly important, the victims of sexual harassment are more likely to be willing to give evidence to support management action at the internal disciplinary stage and at any Industrial Tribunal hearing.

Summary on problem areas

Many of these problem areas inter-relate. In practice they usually work for the benefit of under-performing or misbehaving employees by reducing the likelihood of dismissal. However, when these issues emerge in an Industrial Tribunal they are often taken by the Tribunal as creating injustice upon the employee. Most sensible health service employers are now putting considerable effort into introducing shorter and simpler systems for dealing with discipline, performance failings and the termination of employment.

DISMISSAL FOR ILL HEALTH AND ABSENCE CONTROL

There is a natural sympathy in the health service for sick employees. In addition, health service employees engaged under GWC Conditions of Service benefit from some of the best sick pay entitlements available in Britain. An employee with over five years service will be entitled to six months of full pay followed by six months half pay.

The intention that ill employees should be dealt with sympathetically and the fact that they have significant sick pay entitlements, should not mean that absence is not properly monitored. There are employees who feign or exaggerate ill health in order to increase their annual leave entitlement. Action can and should be taken against them long before they reach their maximum sick pay level. Any employee showing a higher than average level of sick pay, or a peculiar pattern of sickness absence – for example days near to weekends, should be identified and considered. If necessary the employer can request that the employee submit to a medical examination and report in order to determine whether or not there is some underlying medical condition and, if so, what can be done to alleviate it.

In cases of absence a procedure of counselling and warnings should be adopted even if there is no evidence to suggest that misconduct is involved – in other words even if it appears that the absences are genuine. An employee with a high level of short absences can be fairly dismissed long before his or her sick leave entitlement has been exhausted.

A different category of sick employee is the employee with a long period of absence for a single condition. Clearly, such an employee is not capable of his or her work and therefore a fair dismissal may be possible. The long period of sick pay entitlement under Whitley Council terms has an impact here since a Tribunal will usually expect the employer not to dismiss an employee until he or she has exhausted that entitlement, even if it is clear from an early stage that it is highly unlikely that the employee will recover.

Once a long term sick employee has exhausted the sick pay entitlement it would normally be sensible for the employer to act promptly to consider whether or not the employment should continue since the employee will already have been away for a considerable period of time and the absence, coupled with the inability to replace them permanently, will already be creating dislocation in the employee's workplace. However, the mere fact that the employee has exhausted his or her rights will not justify a dismissal – after all the employee might be just about to recover. If recovery in the near future is likely or possible, then certainly it will be difficult to dismiss fairly unless there are overwhelming circumstances requiring an immediate replacement of the employee.

Of course, an employee with long term sickness may well be entitled to an ill health retirement pension which may make the severance more acceptable to the employee than otherwise would have been the case.

Any dismissal for ill health reasons should only take place after adequate medical advice has been obtained. It is vital to ensure that the doctor reporting has an appropriate specialism and is fully briefed as to the nature of the employee's duties. The doctor should be told that the employee's continuing employment is under consideration (so that the doctor realises how serious the matter is) and should be asked to advise upon whether recovery is likely, if so when, and whether recovery will be complete or not. If appropriate, the doctor should be asked to advise on what alternative duties the employee might be capable of. In suitable cases, the question of whether or not the employee's previous duties actually contributed to the health problems should be examined since if they did, having the employee back on that job would not be a sensible choice.

TRADE UNION REPRESENTATION AND RECOGNITION

The health service workforce is heavily unionised and most health service employers recognise a large number of trade unions. This of course has advantages and disadvantages. In the context of termination of employment, recognised trade unions have a major role to play in connection with collective termination, whether on grounds of redundancy or organisational change or to achieve change in terms and conditions of employment. In all those circumstances there is in fact a legal obligation upon the employer to notify and consult with Trade Unions (section 195 of the Trade Union and Labour Relations (Consolidation) Act 1992 as amended by the Trade Union Reform and Employment Rights Act 1993).

It has been decided by the European Court of Justice in *Commission of the European Communities v United Kingdom of Great Britain and Northern Ireland*,[4] that European Directive No. 75/129/EEC requires employers to consult not only with recognised trade unions but, even if no union is recognised, also with any consultative body that exists. Further, if none exists, strictly speaking workers should be invited to nominate representatives. UK law only requires consultation with recognised trade unions and therefore, for the moment, the majority of UK employers can ignore this European obligation. However, the Directive almost certainly applies directly to 'emanations of the state', which phrase includes all NHS employers. Whilst NHS employers almost universally recognise trade unions, there may be certain categories of employee in respect of which a union is not recognised and if so, the obligation to negotiate with other representatives of workers should be borne in mind.

Even with individual terminations, Trade Union involvement is likely. Whilst this may make it harder and slower to take action in relation to particular employees, once an employee has been dismissed, the fact that a union was involved usually makes it easier for the Tribunal to reject a claim for unfair dismissal since the involvement of the Union will have ensured that the employee's case is fully explored.

Employers should be wary of doing deals with Trade Union representatives on disciplinary matters – employees are entitled to have their personal cases considered and to be present when that occurs. Decisions about individual employees should be management decisions, having heard what the employee and the union have to say, rather than deals negotiated between the employer and the union.

SPECIAL ADVANTAGES ENJOYED BY THE HEALTH SERVICE IN RELATION TO DISMISSAL

Health service employees are entitled to redundancy payments which, in comparative terms, are generous. In addition, section 46 of the GWC Conditions of Service and the NHS Superannuation Scheme provide for enhanced pension entitlement in cases of early retirement on grounds of redundancy, organisational change or otherwise in the interests of the service. These arrangements make it much easier than in many other organisations to bring employment of long service employees and they can often be used creatively to deal with a wide variety of problems, particularly with under-performing or unco-operative employees. Further detail *supra*.

The Superannuation Scheme retirement benefits for ill health retirement are also relevant to this topic and are also dealt with earlier in this chapter.

---

[4]   C-383/92 [1994] IRLR 413 ECJ.

CHAPTER 8

SPECIAL PROCEDURES FOR DISCIPLINING AND DISMISSING CONSULTANTS

INTRODUCTION

Discipline and capability are two of the most sensitive and difficult issues that can arise in the workplace. In the context of hospital and community doctors these issues assume a factual and legal complexity which is equalled in few, if any, sectors.

It is commonly thought that the existing procedures are inadequate and inappropriate for dealing with the serious problems that can and do arise. The criticisms include not only complexity but acrimony, sensitivity, time consumption, unwillingness of colleagues to participate in enquiries, enormous expense and excessive legalism.

Nevertheless the current procedures are collectively agreed and form part of practitioners' contracts of employment. Failure to adhere to the relevant provisions would almost certainly cause the proceedings to be seriously delayed (or even abandoned) and potentially expose the employer to the use of injunctions ensuring proper compliance.

Many NHS Trusts are facing these problems for the first time. The Trust is now the employer of many of the practitioners who were previously employed by the Regional Health Authority. The Trusts therefore presently adopt the existing procedures when they assume the practitioner's contract of employment. There is also an opportunity for Trusts to develop new procedures to replace the procedures described below. This chapter will also consider the issues that the Trust should bear in mind when intending to structure and negotiate new procedures to deal with these difficult issues. NHS Trusts are at liberty to negotiate local procedures for dealing with doctors discipline and dismissal. When negotiating new procedures it may be useful to bear in mind the perceived failings of the present procedure.

This is an area of discipline where above all it is essential to be familiar with relevant agreements and departmental guidance.

Much of the guidance requires modification since it was drafted at a time when the practitioners' contracts of employment were not made with NHS Trusts. As a result, NHS Trust and medical directors and personnel departments may be relatively unfamiliar with the procedural details.

This chapter will attempt to provide an introduction to this area by providing guidance to the various existing procedures within which the problems must be handled.

WHAT PROCEDURES ARE THERE FOR HANDLING DOCTORS' DISCIPLINARY ISSUES?

There are five main procedures applicable to senior hospital doctors and dentists. These procedures also apply to community doctors and dentists. The procedures are set down in various departmental circulars which will be explained in greater detail during this chapter.

In summary, disciplinary problems must be placed in one of the following four categories:

Personal misconduct

There are no special procedures for dealing with hospital practitioners in respect of allegations of personal misconduct (see below for definition). NHS employers should therefore operate their own internal local procedures in the same way as they apply to all other categories of staff.

Professional misconduct/incompetence

There are three available procedures depending on the seriousness of the allegations that are under consideration:

- The Professional Review Machinery – should be invoked where it is alleged that a practitioner is persistently failing to carry out his/her contractual commitments to NHS work. This is a pre-disciplinary procedure.

- The Intermediate Procedure – should be invoked in respect of allegations of professional misconduct/incompetence considered insufficiently serious to involve dismissal.

- The HC (90) (9) Annex B procedure – should be invoked in respect of allegations of professional misconduct/incompetence considered sufficiently serious that dismissal could result.

All three procedures are contained in the Department of Health Circular HC (90) (9) issued in March 1990. This circular is based largely on the recommendations of a Joint Working Party (consisting of representatives of the Health Department, the NHS and the professions) which reported in August 1988. The Working Party's remit was to review the existing disciplinary procedures for hospital and community doctors and dentists in the light of the general acknowledgement of the inadequacies of the pre-existing procedures.

The Professional Review Machinery and the Intermediate Procedure were both new introductions following the Working Party's recommendation. They are specifically designed to fill the gap which previously existed whereby the only available procedure for handling any matter of professional misconduct or incompetence was the Serious Disciplinary Procedure (formerly set out in HC 61 (112)).

Prior to the introduction of the two new procedures, employing authorities had either to adopt a procedure often far more comprehensive and cumbersome than the proposed disciplinary action merited; or to wait until matters got so serious that dismissal could be contemplated.

The two new procedures were therefore adopted to allow the employer to manage these issues more effectively.

Professional misconduct/incompetence arising from mental health or physical disability

This is a special procedure which should be invoked where the proposed disciplinary action is contemplated with a view to preventing harm to patients that might be caused by a mental or physical disability from which a doctor is suffering.

This procedure might therefore be appropriate where a consultant continued to practice whilst suffering from a highly contagious disease in circumstances where there was an unacceptable risk of contamination.

This procedure is contained in a separate circular HC (S2) 13. It is often referred to colloquially as 'the three wise men procedure'.

Appeals against dismissal

Paragraph 190 of the Terms and Conditions of Service of Hospital Medical and Dental Staff enshrines a right of appeal against dismissal to the Secretary of State for Health.

The right does not apply to all dismissals (dismissal on the grounds of personal misconduct for example is excluded); nor does it apply to all grades of doctor. The excluded categories and the details of paragraph 190 are considered below.

In all cases where there is no right of appeal to the Secretary of State the practitioner will have to rely on the Local Appeals Procedure. In such cases the constitution of the appeal panel is modified accordingly.

HOW DO I DECIDE INTO WHICH CATEGORY TO PLACE THE MISCONDUCT/INCOMPETENCE IN ORDER TO INVOKE THE CORRECT PROCEDURE?

Since the various procedures are part of a practitioner's contract of employment failure to identify the correct procedure may result in the practitioner having a claim for wrongful and/or unfair dismissal (these terms are fully explained in Chapter 6). These claims are not only likely to be substantial in value but may also result in the Trust incurring considerable legal costs.

It is therefore vital to ensure that misconduct or incompetence is properly categorised from the outset of the disciplinary process.

The problem of properly defining the allegation in question is one of great practical difficulty. It is one also of great practical importance particularly in the light of the differences in the appeals procedures which depend on the classification of the allegations.

Circular HC (90) (9) contains certain definitions which are agreed guidance between the department and the professions.

What is personal misconduct?

HC (90) (9) has the following agreed definition of personal misconduct:

'Performance or behaviour of practitioners due to factors other than those associated with the exercise of medical or dental skills.'

The following are relatively clear examples of personal misconduct within this definition:

- theft of NHS property;
- fraudulent expenses claims;
- racial/sexual harassment of fellow employees;
- use of violence.

What is professional misconduct?

Circular HC (90) (9) provides the following guidance:

'Performance or behaviour of practitioner arising from the exercise of medical or dental skills.'

The following are examples of professional misconduct:

- rudeness towards patients;

- unco-operative attitude towards colleagues eg unsympathetic attitudes towards patients, patronising towards nursing staff;

- refusal to participate in team development plan.

What is professional incompetence?

Circular HC (90) (9) provides the following guidance:

'Adequacy of performance of Practitioners related to the exercise of their medical or dental skills and professional judgement.'

The emphasis on this category is on carrying out clinical skills. The following are examples:

- negligent examination before treatment;

- failure to carry out proper examination;

- improper diagnosis;

- failure to keep adequate records;

- technical errors in surgery.

Are there any special considerations that apply when operating local procedures in relation to doctors who allegedly have personally misconducted themselves?

Yes – although it is agreed that practitioners should be subject to the same treatment as any other NHS staff if disciplinary action is taken in respect of personal misconduct, the following considerations should be borne in mind:

- Local procedures should be drafted so that they include doctors and dentists adequately.

- Section 40 of the General Whitley Terms and Conditions of Service apply equally to practitioners. These are national guidelines specifying that in any serious matter (other than gross misconduct where summary dismissal might be justified) employees must first be reprimanded and given a formal warning. Employees would only be dismissed if the offence was repeated after a warning had been given. Further, these guidelines provide that senior professional staff, including consultants, can be dismissed only by decision of the full employing authority. Clearly in relation to NHS Trusts an appropriate modification has to be made.

- Section 40 also lays down guidelines on appeal procedures. It will be recalled that there is generally no right of appeal to the Secretary of State under paragraph 190 if a dismissal is on the grounds of personal misconduct. HC (90) (9) supplements section 40 by providing that there should be a specially constituted appeal panel to hear an appeal by a practitioner who has been dismissed for personal misconduct.

- It is recommended that the appeal panel be made up of the chairman of the employing body, a practitioner who is a member of the employing body and another practitioner in the same or associated speciality as the practitioner involved (but who would normally be employed in a different body).

- In respect of mixed personal and professional misconduct the right of appeal under paragraph 190 is retained provided that the allegation which leads to the dismissal contains elements of both personal misconduct and professional misconduct. A practitioner may also claim that the classification by the employing body of the action as personal misconduct is unreasonable. As discussed below if the practitioner is successful then the right of appeal under paragraph 190 to the Secretary of State is retained.

THE PROFESSIONAL REVIEW MACHINERY HC (90) (9) ANNEX D

The Professional Review is undertaken by a standing panel normally consisting of the chairman of the Medical Staff Committee and two other consultants, one full-time and one part-time. Whenever the panel hears a case a fourth member from a suitable speciality is co-opted from another employing body.

When is the professional review machinery appropriate?

This procedure is designed as an informal pre-disciplinary mechanism with the objective of nipping problems in the bud.

Like the Intermediate procedure, this procedure was introduced in the 1990 Circular. The Professional Review Machinery is an attempt to introduce peer group pressure on those practitioners who it is alleged are repeatedly failing to honour their contractual commitments. Typical examples might include missing ward rounds or clinics.

Who can initiate the review?

There is no restriction as to who can refer an allegation to the panel.

Practitioners and the Medical Director may refer an allegation directly to the panel. All other staff should direct their complaint through their Line Manager who in turn is obliged to refer the complaint to the Medical Director.

All referrals must be in writing. The complainant has the right to remain anonymous.

What form does the review take?

If the Medical Director considers an allegation appropriate for referral to the panel, the practitioner concerned is informed of the referral verbally by the Chairman of the panel. The practitioner is also provided with a copy of the written referral.

The practitioner is then invited to an informal meeting with the panel at which the allegation is discussed.

If the panel considers that the allegation is unfounded then no further action is taken. If the panel find that there is some substance in the allegation the practitioner is advised by the panel and a second review meeting is arranged to take place within six months.

If after the second meeting there is no improvement or if the practitioner declines to meet the panel, the matter is referred to the Medical Director.

At that stage the Medical Director may decide to invoke an appropriate disciplinary procedure.

What records are kept of the panel meetings?

The Chairman of the panel keeps a note of the fact that a meeting has been held which records only the nature of the allegation or whether the practitioner has been advised by the panel.

Is a complainant exposed to defamation proceedings?

There are special provisions designed to ensure that referrals can be made with immunity from civil actions.

The complainant may well be able to rely on the defence of 'qualified privilege' in respect of any defamation claims. This defence applies to any statement made pursuant to a moral, legal or social duty provided that the statement is made to a person who has a corresponding duty to receive it. Further, Annex D contains a recommendation that the employing body should indemnify a complainant who has acted in good faith against any costs and damages the complainant becomes liable to pay.

This is clearly designed to encourage genuine complaints to emerge free from the threat of exposure to civil proceedings.

When is the intermediate procedure appropriate?

The purpose of this procedure is to provide the employing body with a mechanism to deal at an early stage with those cases of alleged professional misconduct/incompetence which are sufficiently serious to warrant some form of disciplinary action but insufficiently serious to lead to dismissal.

The Intermediate Procedure is therefore to be invoked when the employing body has to deal with relatively serious allegations that cannot be resolved through informal means.

This procedure is not restricted to disciplinary situations. It is also designed to deal with professional differences of opinion that may be causing problems within a given department.

Who can initiate the procedure?

There is no restriction on the source of any allegations. Nurses, consultants and presumably patients can refer a complaint to the medical director.

If the medical director is satisfied that it is appropriate to deal with the allegation under the intermediate procedure, what form does the intermediate procedure take?

The Medical Director informs the Joint Consultants Committee about the problem and the JCC is asked to nominate two appropriate assessors from a different employing body. The JCC will constitute the panel after taking into account the nature of the allegations and considering the specialities of the practitioner concerned.

What form does the assessment take?

Once nominated the assessors should receive within one month a detailed statement of case from the Medical Director. This statement is also copied to the practitioner(s) concerned.

The Assessors may in the light of detailed statements review the suitability of the intermediate procedure for dealing with the allegations.

If the Assessors consider that it is appropriate for the intermediate procedure then the Assessors have general powers to determine who they wish to interview by way of investigating the allegations.

However, they have no power to compel any one to co-operate with the investigation. Any one who is interviewed is expected to give a written statement or to sign a written record of any interview.

Although the Assessors are entitled to the appropriate secretarial and administrative support to facilitate their investigation, there is no provision in the guidance for any fee to be paid.

What right do the practitioners have during the assessment?

The practitioner is entitled to the following during the assessment:

- to be informed of the Medical Director's decision to invoke the intermediate procedure;

- to receive a copy of the statement of case prepared for the Assessors by the Medical Director;

- to receive a copy of the list of those witnesses the Assessors intend to interview;

- to be interviewed if the practitioner so chooses;

- to receive a copy of all written statements and interview records provided by the interviewees;

- to meet personally with the assessors and to be accompanied by a representative of their professional organisation, or by a friend;

- to receive part one of the Assessor's report (see below);

- to comment within 14 days on the factual findings in part one of the report.

What are the assessors required to do?

The Assessors are required to prepare a report in two distinct parts:

Part 1 – sets out the Assessors' factual findings. This part is sent to both the Medical Director and the practitioner in question.

Part 2 – contains the Assessors' view as to whether the practitioner was at fault. This part may contain the Assessors' recommendations on organisational matters within the department and any advice to be given to the practitioner. This part is not sent to the practitioner.

The Assessors do not make any recommendations on whether disciplinary action would be appropriate and they have no disciplinary powers.

Who decides whether disciplinary action will be taken?

It is for the Medical Director to decide whether or not the assessment merits disciplinary action being taken. If action is to be taken against the practitioner this must be taken in accordance with the locally agreed disciplinary procedure applicable to all staff.

Specific reference is made in the circular to the ACAS Code of Practice and the principles of section 40 GWC.

How should any appeal against disciplinary action be handled?

There are also specific guidelines for the constitution of the appeal committee. These are the same as discussed above in relation to appeals against disciplinary action on the ground of personal misconduct.

SERIOUS CASES OF PROFESSIONAL MISCONDUCT OR INCOMPETENCE HC (90) (9) ANNEX B

This procedure has remained largely unaltered since 1961. The present circular introduced a small number of changes without altering the essential provisions of the previous guidance set out in HN (61) 112. The changes were designed to reduce the length and expense of disciplinary action. It is doubtful whether or not any real progress has been made.

When is this procedure appropriate?

This procedure should be invoked to deal with serious disciplinary charges relating to allegations of professional misconduct or professional incompetence.

In particular this procedure should be invoked where it is contemplated that the outcome of disciplinary action could be the dismissal of the practitioner.

What power is there to suspend?

The employing body retains the same power to suspend a practitioner as in respect of any other member of staff who is faced with serious disciplinary action. However, the employing body will have to pay the practitioner throughout any period of suspension as well as, in appropriate circumstances, fund a locum.

What time limits are imposed?

There is specific guidance on the time within which the various stages under this procedure should be completed. Reference is therefore made to the prescribed time limits applicable to each stage of the process. Reference is also made below to the prescribed time limits applicable to each stage of the process. The starting point is that the majority of cases should be completed within a period of 32 weeks beginning with the identification of a *prima facie* case.

There are four principal stages to the procedure:

- The Preliminary Investigation.
- The Factual Enquiry.
- The Enquiry Panel Report.
- The Employing Body's Decision.

What form does a preliminary investigation take?

The Medical Director assisted if necessary by the Trust's legal advisor carries out preliminary enquiries to establish whether there is a *prima facie* case which could result in serious disciplinary action.

If it is decided to undertake a preliminary enquiry then the practitioner has the following rights:

- to be warned immediately in writing of the nature of the allegation;
- to be formally advised that an enquiry is being considered;
- to receive copies of all relevant correspondence;
- to have all comments s/he may have, considered as part of the preliminary investigations;
- to be given reasonable time to make representations and to seek advice if a final decision is taken to proceed.

The practitioner has four weeks to provide his comments on the allegation(s).

Thereafter a decision to proceed should be made within two weeks.

Does there always have to be an enquiry by an investigatory panel?

No – broadly the role of the investigatory panel is to decide the facts. If the facts are either undisputed or have already been established then there is no requirement for an enquiry.

The enquiry will usually be unnecessary where, for example, the facts have already been established by a public inquiry or in a court of law which has found the practitioner guilty of a criminal charge arising out of the same allegation(s) being considered by the employer.

If a panel is to be appointed this should be done within three months of a decision to proceed.

If an enquiry is held what form does it take?

The panel sits in private. A list of witnesses is drawn up with the main points of evidence that it is intended each witness will give.

The enquiry is extremely legalistic for a disciplinary procedure. Witnesses are examined and cross-examined. The Chairman of the enquiry has the discretion to determine the admissibility of evidence and in many respects it is not dissimilar to an Industrial Tribunal:

- The doctor has the right of personal appearance and is entitled to hear all of the evidence that is given.

- The timescale within which the enquiry should be completed is one week.

- The employing body has a period of three months within which the panel should be appointed.

What form does the enquiry's report take?

Within four weeks of the hearing being concluded the enquiry should report its finding.

The report is divided into two separate parts:

Part one – sets out the panel's factual findings. These findings are sent to the practitioner.

Part two – states the panel's view as to whether or not the practitioner has been at fault.

If the employing body so requests the panel is empowered in part two to recommend disciplinary action.

The panel has no power to take disciplinary action in respect of the practitioner.

Who takes any decision in relation to dismissal?

It is for the employing body to take this decision. Within four weeks of the practitioner having made comments on part one of the panel's report the employing body must make its decision.

A meeting is arranged with the practitioner if the panel's report has indicated that the practitioner is considered to be at fault.

The practitioner has the right to receive part two of the report at this stage. He should receive this part in good time before the meeting at which disciplinary action is taken.

He is given the opportunity at the meeting to make any plea in mitigation he sees fit before a final decision is taken.

APPEAL TO SECRETARY OF STATE UNDER PARAGRAPH 190 OF THE MEDICAL AND DENTAL WHITLEY COUNCIL (HC (90) (9) ANNEX C)

This is the right of appeal to the Secretary of State against dismissal if a practitioner considers his appointment has been unfairly terminated. This right of appeal is not available to all practitioners.

What are the qualifying conditions that a practitioner must fulfil in order to be able to appeal to the Secretary of State?

The right is limited to those practitioners who have been dismissed for professional misconduct or incompetence. Accordingly a dismissal on the grounds of personal misconduct will not carry with it the right of appeal to the Secretary of State. Any appeal in relation to a practitioner dismissed for personal misconduct would have to be under the employing body's own disciplinary procedures which themselves should comply with section 40 GWC.

The right of appeal to the Secretary of State only applies to certain grades of practitioner.

Only those who are SHMO, SHDO, Associate Specialists, Transferred Child Psychiatrists and Hospital Practitioners have this right to appeal.

Finally, there are certain restrictions in terms of the number of hours per week that a practitioner works. Only those practitioners whose contractual commitments are for more than six NHDs per week may have a right of appeal to the Secretary of State regardless of the reason for their dismissal. The right may also apply to practitioners who have no other NHS medical income equal to or greater than the income they receive from the appointment which has been terminated.

This qualifying condition may be subject to review in the light of recent developments in the law relating to equal opportunities which established discrimination against part-timers and was *prima facie* contrary to European law.

What happens in cases of mixed personal/professional competence?

A practitioner is entitled to challenge whether his dismissal is solely in relation to personal misconduct. The right of appeal is retained under paragraph 190 to the Secretary of State if the reason for dismissal is part personal and part professional misconduct. A practitioner may also claim that his employer's classification of the allegation to personal misconduct is unreasonable and, if that challenge is successful retain the right of appeal to the Secretary of State.

The right to challenge the classification is set out in paragraph 190 (d) and (e).

The practitioner must invoke the challenge within one month of receiving the notice of termination of his employment.

The Secretary of State is then obliged to refer the issue to a panel who must determine whether the dismissal is solely on the ground of personal misconduct.

The panel is constituted in accordance with paragraph 190 (e) of the relevant version of paragraph 190.

If the panel decides that the dismissal was not on the sole ground of personal misconduct then the practitioner has one month to exercise his right of appeal under paragraph 190 to the Secretary of State. Thereafter the appeal will continue under the procedural provisions generally applicable to the paragraph.

WHEN MUST THE NOTICE BE SERVED TO EXERCISE THIS RIGHT OF APPEAL?

A practitioner may serve a notice of appeal to the Secretary of State at any time during his/her period of notice.

The right of appeal to the Secretary of State does not apply in cases of summary dismissal (*Guirgus v Trent Regional Health Authority* (1990)).

The practitioner must send a full statement of facts of the case to the Secretary of State within four months of receipt of notice of termination. There is discretion to extend the period within which the statement of facts must be served if it was not reasonably practicable for the practitioner to comply with the four months time limit.

The Secretary of State then requires the employing body to present its own views on the case. The employing body has two months to comply with that request. Again there is a reasonable practicability extension.

How is the appeal panel constituted?

Once both views have been received the Secretary of State appoints a professional committee.

The professional committee is constituted as follows:

- the Chief Medical officer or Deputy who chairs the committee;
- departmental representatives;
- nominated representatives of the joint consultant's committee.

The professional committee is normally assisted by a legal advisor.

If the committee sees fit it interviews the practitioner. This should be between one and three months after receipt of the employing body's views on the case.

Both parties are entitled to full legal representation before the committee.

What recommendation does the professional committee make?

The Professional committee has power to take one of three options:

- to confirm the termination;
- to direct that the practitioner's employment should continue;
- a third solution agreeable to both parties.

The Secretary of State takes the decision on the basis of the recommendations of the professional committee. A typical third solution might be allowing the practitioner to continue under supervision.

Is the practitioner entitled to pay throughout the proceedings?

Paragraph 190 appeals are notoriously lengthy. If an appeal is lodged the notice of dismissal has no effect until the appeal is determined. What this means is that the employee continues to be employed and paid until the appeal is finally determined.

CHAPTER 9

NOTICE OF TERMINATION, FIXED TERM CONTRACTS AND PAY IN LIEU OF NOTICE

ORDINARY CONTRACTS

Most employees are employed on 'permanent' or 'indefinite' contracts, that is to say contracts with no specified end date which will continue until the employer gives the employee notice of termination or the employee gives the employer notice of resignation. Such contracts also terminate in certain other, less frequent, circumstances such as the death of the employee.

So far as notice is concerned, the obligation of each party to give notice is governed by the contract of employment. If the contract expressly states a period of notice that is required to be given by any particular party, then that period will apply, subject to the statutory minimum referred to below.

If the contract does not expressly specify a period of notice then a period will be implied by common law (as opposed to statute law). If most employees in a particular category do have an expressly stated notice period but, through some oversight, the particular employee does not, then that standard period will be implied by law. If there is no implied period of notice for the category of employees with that particular employer then the Courts will imply a term of 'reasonable notice'. Usually reasonable notice will be a period not less than the pay interval so that a monthly paid employee will be entitled to receive and obliged to give one month's notice. However, with more senior and specialist staff a longer period of notice may be implied, for example three, six or even 12 months. It is careless to leave this issue to implication.

For many years now statute law has provided for minimum periods of notice and for ordinary employees these are tending to supplant the periods that would otherwise have been implied in a case where the contract did not specify the period. The minima are currently set out in section 49 of the Employment Protection (Consolidation) Act 1978. An employer must given any employee who has been continuously employed for one month or more not less than one week's notice of termination. This minimum is increased with service, the entitlement being to one week's notice for each year of continuous employment until 12 weeks notice is reached which is the highest statutory minimum. An employee who has been continuously employed for one month or more is required to give not less than one week's notice of termination to the employer.

The consequences of not giving the notice required are examined later in this chapter.

FIXED TERM AND PURPOSE OR EVENT CONTRACTS

Some employees are engaged on contracts that will come to an end automatically. The first category of these is contracts where the termination date can be ascertained right from the outset. Lawyers call these contracts 'fixed term contracts' but in ordinary parlance this phrase is usually reserved for contracts with a fixed end date that are to last for at least a year. The phrase that is usually used to describe shorter fixed term contracts is 'temporary contracts'.

There is no magic in these phrases. The key point is that the duration of the contract is known from the outset so that the contract will come to an end of its own accord when the duration is complete. Consequently, notice of termination is not required. Some such contracts additionally provide that either party or both parties can terminate the contract during its fixed period by notice. For legal purposes such a contract is still a fixed term contract.

The 'short term rolling contracts' issued to general managers pursuant to advice issued by the Secretary of State in May 1986 are a kind of fixed term contract. They provide for a minimum initial period of three, four or five years with the contract being reviewed 24 months before its expiry with a view to renewals then being granted on an annual basis. The clause recommended in the advice is not well drafted since it is ambiguous about whether the renewed contracts should be for a fixed term of one year or for a longer fixed term.

The same advice recommends that Health Service employers should ensure that any manager employed on these terms contracts out of his or her rights under section 54 of the EPCA to claim unfair dismissal, and the advice also states that section 45 of the GWC Conditions of Service, which deals with redundancy payments, does not apply. Because of changes since 1986 it is now in fact vital to ensure that the contracting out refers not only to unfair dismissal under section 54 of the EPCA but also to both the right to a redundancy payment under section 45 and any right to any statutory redundancy payment.

A second category of fixed term contract should more strictly be called a minimum term contract since it states that there is a minimum period of employment and, thereafter, the employment can be terminated on a certain amount of notice given by one party to the other. This kind of contract is rare in the Health Service but very common in the private sector since it gives a new recruit some security that he or she will not lose employment soon after joining the new employer.

It is extremely common to see contracts that were intended to include some kind of fixed term together with some ability to give notice of termination which are very badly drafted. In such cases it is often not at all clear what the parties intended. Great care should be taken to get the wording right.

The final category of contract with a special duration provision consists of 'purpose' and 'event' contracts. A purpose contract states that the employment is to last so long as is necessary for some particular purpose to be fulfilled, for example until practical completion of the construction of a new hospital. An event contract is one that is specified to last until some particular event occurs, for example until a specified ward is closed. Purpose and event contracts last until the purpose is completed or the event has occurred. They then come to an end automatically without the need for either party to serve notice on the other. Once again it is possible to specify in such contracts that termination prior to the completion of the purpose or the occurrence of the event can be achieved by notice.

WHAT IS THE VALUE OF FIXED TERM, PURPOSE OR EVENT CONTRACTS?

Such contracts can give considerable security of employment to the employee but they of course carry with them the corresponding risk on the part of the employer that if for whatever reason it does not wish to continue to employ the employee, it will cost a considerable amount to part company unless the contract provides for earlier termination by notice. The second advantage is that such a contract does make it clear to the employee from the start that permanent employment is not guaranteed which helps to avoid ill feeling and recriminations, and the likelihood of Tribunal claims, when the contract does in fact come to an end.

Probably the most important advantage of fixed term, purpose or event contracts is in relation to special rules applying to the law of unfair dismissal. So far as fixed term contracts are concerned, the law provides that non renewal of a fixed term contract is deemed to be a dismissal for the purposes of entitling an employee to claim unfair dismissal (EPCA 1978 section 55). However, if the fixed term is for a minimum of one year the employee can, by signing suitable wording, sign away the right to claim unfair dismissal if the contract is not renewed on expiry. Any dismissal prior to expiry is still protected by the unfair dismissal legislation subject to the employee having sufficient continuity of employment. If the contract is for a fixed period of at least two years the employee can also sign away the right to a redundancy payment on non-renewal.

There are particular traps with contracting out in relation to renewals and extensions of fixed term contracts. These traps stem from two areas of legal doubt. The first is whether the employee must sign the contracting out in any extension of renewal or whether the original contracting out remains effective. Particularly with a redundancy payment it seems that a repeated signature is required and certainly the only safe course of action is to ensure that the employee agrees in writing afresh on every extension or renewal.

The second area of doubt is that it is not clear whether contracting out is valid if the extension or renewal is for less than the relevant minimum fixed term (one year in the case of unfair dismissal and two years in the case of redundancy payments). The current state of the law appears to be that if there are any changes between the terms of the old contract and the terms of the new contract then the new contract must be for the specified minimum period, but that if there is an extension which is merely a postponement of the termination date of the original contract, it may be that the contracting out remains valid even though the extension is for less than the specified minimum period. Once again the prudent advice is to extend or renew where possible for the relevant minimum period and, if this is not practicable, to ensure that there are no new terms agreed in the extended or renewed period and to so phrase the documentation as to indicate that one is extending the original fixed term rather than creating a new or additional one.

For purpose or event contracts the position is even more dramatic – the expiry of a contract on completion of the purpose or on the occurrence of the event is not a dismissal at all. This means that the employee cannot claim unfair dismissal and is not entitled to a redundancy payment. In certain circumstances therefore, a purpose or event contract may be a very attractive proposition. However, since it does not carry with it statutory protection against unfair dismissal and redundancy, employers should be aware that Industrial Tribunals are likely to look hard at any contract alleged to be one of this kind and may well find facts to support a conclusion either that it was a contract terminable by notice in the ordinary way or that it was in truth a fixed term contract.

For example, if the purpose or event is in effect that the employment will continue until the end of a contract under which the employer has to supply a service to a purchaser for a particular period, it is quite likely that the Tribunal will find that the contract of employment was in truth a fixed term contract since its end date could be ascertained at the outset.

Any employer seeking to rely upon a purpose or event contract would be well advised to spell out to the employee at the outset that there will be no right to claim unfair dismissal or a redundancy payment on completion since this will help a Tribunal to reach the conclusion that there should be no remedy.

The consequences of terminating a fixed term or purpose or event contract prior to its natural expiry are considered below.

TERMINATION IN BREACH OF CONTRACT

If an employee is given notice of dismissal, or gives notice of resignation, and that notice period is served out, then no breach of contract occurs. There may be an entitlement to a redundancy payment, and the employee may claim unfair dismissal, but the employee is entitled to no remedy in respect of the *contract* because there has been no breach of the contract. The same is true in the case of a fixed term contract which expires and is not renewed.

However it very frequently happens that a contract is brought to an end in circumstances which do amount to a breach. Lawyers call this 'wrongful dismissal' to distinguish it from the very different concept of unfair dismissal. The most everyday example is a case of immediate termination with 'pay in lieu of notice'. Technically, in such a case the employer has broken the contract by not giving the notice of termination required under it, but then tenders to the employee as compensation the amount that the employee would have earned during the notice period had proper notice been given.

Another example of termination in breach of contract would be where the employer purports to dismiss the employee summarily for gross misconduct, but in the end a court or tribunal holds that there was no gross misconduct. A third example is where the disciplinary procedure is incorporated into the employee's contract of employment and the employee is dismissed without that procedure having been observed properly.

The final example is where the employee resigns, claiming that the conduct of the employer amounts to a breach of contract of such seriousness that the employee is entitled to rescind the contract without notice (the employee may nevertheless give notice if he or she wishes). Such a situation is usually called a 'constructive dismissal', a phrase that arose after the introduction of the legislation against unfair dismissal since a resignation of this kind is treated as a dismissal in order to allow an employee to bring a claim for unfair dismissal. From the contractual point of view, the employee is resigning because of the employer's serious breach and is therefore entitled to damages.

WHAT IS THE MEASURE OF LOSS?

This topic has been addressed in circulars TEL(94)2 and AHG(94)18 issued by the NHS Management Executive in May 1994. In this section we shall examine the general law that applies and then comment on some specific aspects of the NHSME guidance. Health service employers should also read the relevant circular.

If a contract is terminated in a manner that is in breach of contract, then the employee is entitled to compensation for what he or she has lost until the date when the contract could first have been terminated without breach. In the case of a contract that can be terminated by notice, obviously that period is the length of the notice period. In the case of a fixed term contract, the period is the time until the expiry date of the contract. It will readily be seen that in the case of employees with relatively short notice periods, the compensation available is likely to be low and the employee is likely to recover more through the remedy of unfair dismissal – if the dismissal can be shown to be one that is unfair within the meaning of the Employment Protection (Consolidation) Act 1978.

The employee is entitled to compensation for what he or she has lost. This will usually be calculated by reference to average take home pay, in other words after the deduction of tax and National Insurance (*Parsons v BNM Laboratories Ltd* (1963)[1]). Since payment in lieu of notice of this kind is technically damages for breach of contract, it is not an 'emolument' of the employment and consequently is not liable to income tax unless the level of £30,000 is reached, at which point special tax rules apply to tax the excess at the employee's current marginal rate of tax. Similarly money in lieu of notice is not earnings for the purposes of National Insurance.

For these reasons, many employers, when calculating pay in lieu of notice, will work on the gross value of average pay before tax and National Insurance, but technically only the net amount need be paid, the balance not being payable to either the employee or the Inland Revenue. In the case of long notice periods, the difference will be significant and employers such as NHS Trusts need to be mindful of their legal obligations not to expend money unnecessarily. However, with ordinary employees on ordinary periods of notice, it is often a good idea to pay the gross amount since to fail to do so quite often provokes claims, such as unfair dismissal, that otherwise would not have been brought.

It should be noted that if the contract of employment gives the employer the express right to terminate the employment with immediate effect and pay in lieu of notice then such a payment is an emolument and tax and National Insurance contributions are due on it. It is the authors' view that section 60 of the GWC Conditions of Service does not create such a right so that if the contract merely refers to the GWC on the question of notice there should be no problem about tax. However, the Inland Revenue has been known to take the opposite view.

It should also be noted that to serve notice and say that the employee need not attend work during the notice period does *not* prevent pay during the notice period being an emolument and thus subject to tax and National Insurance. This can occur accidentally, for example, if the employer wrote on 31 May 'Your employment is terminated and you will be paid in lieu of three months notice. Your last day of service will be 31 August'. Such a letter would strongly suggest that full notice was being given and the 'payments in lieu' would be taxable as ordinary pay.

The general principle that pay in lieu of notice is compensation for losses suffered means that if the employee finds other work then the take home

---

1   [1963] All ER 658.

value of that other employment must be deducted from the compensation Pound for Pound. Even if the employee has not yet found other work, a reduction can be made if it is anticipated that he or she will find other work within the notice period. Even with senior and specialised staff, the courts are likely to expect an employee to find other work within a year, and accordingly the compensation payable under a contract terminable on two years notice may not be much more, if at all, than the compensation payable in the case of a contract terminable on one year's notice.

The final element that can reduce the amount of compensation is the fact that by being compensated all at once, rather than having to earn the money over a period of time, the employee is receiving the benefit of the interest earned from early receipt of the monies. A discount can be applied for this 'accelerated receipt'. The appropriate figure to apply of course varies with interest rates but the current recommendation from the NHSME is 2.5% per annum. This should be calculated by applying the percentage to the middle date of the payment period over which the compensation has been calculated.

Judging from the reaction to the NHSME guidance on termination payments for general and senior managers, it appears that these principles have come as a shock to many individuals in the Health Service. It appears that a practice has developed of employees receiving their pay in lieu for long periods without deductions for tax, alternative employment etc. There may be occasions when such generosity is appropriate, but it should at least be recognised when making such more generous payments that that is just what they are.

COMPENSATION FOR BENEFITS IN KIND

So far we have been assuming that the employee's only significant contractual benefit is pay. Of course that is very often not the case and the employee is entitled to compensation for the loss of all the benefits due under the contract. Account should therefore be taken of the value, *to the employee*, of benefits such as private use of the employer's motor vehicles, any insurances provided, and loss of pension scheme membership.

TAX ON LARGE TERMINATION PAYMENTS

It was mentioned above that in the case where the termination payment exceeds £30,000 tax is chargeable. This is under section 144 and section 188(4) of the Income and Corporation Taxes Act 1988. All sums and benefits passed to an employee on termination must be included in this calculation, including any redundancy payment or, for example, the value of a car transferred to the employee.

To the extent that the total exceeds £30,000 it will be taxed at the marginal rate of the employee in the tax year of termination. This marginal rate is likely to be 40%, but it could be 25% in some cases. Of course this could result in the employee receiving less after tax than the amount after tax that he or she would have earned had the contract not been terminated in breach of contract. In such a case, the compensation has to be grossed up, so that after this special 'golden handshake' tax has been applied the amount left is the correct compensation sum. The practical application of these principles is dealt with in the ready reckoner issued by the NHSME and referred to below.

THE NHSME READY RECKONER

The ready reckoner published by the NHSME in the circulars referred to above is specially adapted to the Health Service and is therefore particularly useful for calculating termination payments. Although the ready reckoner was published in the context of short term rolling contracts for senior managers, the principles apply to any case of termination in breach of contract.

In the authors' opinion, when using that ready reckoner, managers should, in addition to taking account of the notes attached to them, bear in mind the following points:

1   In the case of employees whose total termination payments do not exceed £30,000, the grossing up section on page three of the ready reckoner items (i) to (iii) can be ignored.

2   On page three of the ready reckoner point (ii) 'Add tax at 40%' could easily be misunderstood. Many people might add 40% of the sum shown in the ready reckoner as 'M' but that would be quite wrong. In fact M should be multiplied by two-thirds to produce the tax, N.

3   The loss of Superannuation benefits referred to on page three of the ready reckoner is added in to the compensation after grossing up for tax in the case of a large termination exceeding £30,000. In fact, since this compensation is taxable also, it should be included in the grossing up exercise by amending the top of page three to read:

    'Total net loss after new remuneration deducted and compensation for lost Superannuation benefits given [see note 8 ...] X + S - Y = Z.'

4   The treatment of what would have been the employee's contributions to the Superannuation Scheme is not entirely accurate. Contrary to what is stated in note eight of the ready reckoner, any employee's contributions to the Superannuation Scheme during the expected period of unemployment should be included, rather than excluded.

CHAPTER 10

ACHIEVING CHANGE TO TERMS OF EMPLOYMENT

INTRODUCTION

Since a contract of employment is an agreement between employer and employee, it can be changed by mutual consent at any time. What if consent is not obtained? Can the employer give notice of changed terms that are to apply, perhaps after expiry of the contractual notice period? This question was decisively settled in 1987 by the House of Lords in the case of *Rigby v Ferodo* (1987).[1] It was held in that case that a purported notice of change of terms and conditions could not be effective: either the parties *agreed* to a change in terms and conditions, or the employer would have to give notice to end, rather than change, the contract of employment. An employer is, of course, free to offer new terms of employment that will apply if the employees accept employment after the existing contracts have come to an end.

Sometimes an employer may decide to force the pace of achieving consent by changing the terms of employment unilaterally and taking the position that if the employees live with those changes, then they can be taken to have agreed with them.

There is one further way in which an employer may be able to make a change in working methods or working conditions. This is where rather than seeking to change the contract, the employer uses an express right in the contract to make such a change. There is no doubt that flexibility clauses reserving the right to make changes in this way can be effective, but the courts police such powers carefully.

In this chapter we look at all these approaches to achieving change in terms and conditions and at the practical and legal considerations that affect the approach of employers seeking to achieve such changes.

ACHIEVING CHANGE BY CONSENT

This must be the preferred option for any sensible employer. In the case of a workforce that is largely unionised, the employer may well seek to achieve a new consensus through negotiation with the union concerned. However, unless contracts of employment expressly or impliedly provide that any terms agreed between the employer and the union shall be incorporated

---

[1]   [1987] 1RLR 516 HL.

automatically into the individual employees' contracts, obtaining the consent of the union is merely a practical precursor to the necessary step of actually obtaining the agreement of each individual employee – each employee after all has his or her individual contract of employment with the employer.

Quite apart from the fact that consensus is better than strife, there is a legal reason for seeking to achieve agreement. The reason is that if agreement cannot be reached, the employer is likely to end up having to achieve the change by dismissal (see below). A dismissal in order to achieve the changes to terms and conditions of employment can be fair, being a dismissal 'for some other substantial reason', provided that the employer can show that it had a good business reason to make the change, that there was full explanation, consultation and negotiation with employees and that the effect on employees' personal lives was taken into account properly. Therefore, even if agreement cannot be reached with employees about the new terms, the fact that agreement has been sought will increase the chances of persuading the Tribunal that the subsequent dismissals were fair.

Apart from the common sense of negotiating with any recognised Trade Union, there is also an obligation derived from European law to negotiate in these circumstances. That obligation arises because the Directive governing redundancy[2] defines redundancy widely and this has been reflected in the UK law on compulsory notification and consultation with recognised trade unions under section 195 of the Trade Union and Labour Relations (Consolidation) Act 1992 as amended by the Trade Union Reform and Employment Rights Act 1993. The definition of 'redundancy' for this purpose only is 'dismissal for a reason not related to the individual concerned'. This therefore includes terminations where there is no reduction in numbers but in order to achieve a change in terms and conditions of employment. Since, if negotiations fail, such terminations are likely, union notification and consultation are a requirement in any case where there is a recognised Trade Union. In fact, where there is no recognised union for the workers concerned, there is probably a duty to negotiate with other representatives of workers.

Most managers will have their own views as to how to reach agreement on issues such as this, which may include identifying a few areas where some compromise can be made during the course of discussions. For the reasons explained below, it is vital for the changes that are required to be clearly spelt out and for the practical consequences of the proposed changes for employees to be explored fully. It is often the case that what appears to be an insignificant and unimportant change is in practice one that causes major personal difficulties for a few employees. It may be necessary to make special arrangements for them or to amend the plans in order to take account of their particular difficulties.

---

2   No 75/129/EEC.

One very common way of achieving agreement with employees to changes that are potentially to their disadvantage, is to couple those changes with the annual pay review. It can be made absolutely clear that the increased rate will be paid only to those who accept the other changes. The main disadvantage of this approach is that some employees may decide that they do not like the proposed changes so much that they may decline the pay rise. This can leave the employer with an awkward situation in which it has employees working under two different sets of terms and conditions. In some cases, such a situation will not merely be awkward but will be quite impossible, for example where changes in shift systems are introduced. In such a case the employer would be prudent to make it clear from the outset that although an increase in pay is offered, the change in terms will be required for all employees (by dismissal and re-employment if necessary – see below) and that there is no option of remaining on existing terms.

The option of coupling changes in terms with a pay review offer is not open in a case where employees are contractually entitled to the pay increase, for example they are employed on Whitley Council terms and the relevant Council has agreed a pay increase.

If an employer does reach agreement with employees as to the new terms, it is vital that those new terms should be recorded in writing and that the employees should sign to confirm their agreement to them. This is much more important than obtaining a signature to terms and conditions when an employee is engaged in the first place because it is vital to be able to prove subsequently that the employee did know what the new terms were and expressly agreed to the changes.

As a matter of contract law, a binding legal contract requires not only agreement but also 'consideration' flowing from employer to employee and from employee to employer. The consideration can be anything given or promised by one party to the other. In a contract of employment the employer provides consideration to the employee by promising to pay and provide certain benefits in kind and the employee provides consideration to the employer by promising to work in accordance with the terms of the contract.

If new terms for existing employees are agreed, it can be argued, if all the changes are on one side, that the other side has given nothing new and has therefore provided no consideration for the new agreement. Without consideration on both sides the agreement is not contractually binding. If such an argument were valid, it would mean that any pay increases given by employers would not be binding since the employee would have given no fresh consideration for them. The general legal view is therefore that in a contract of employment, when new terms are agreed, the renewed promises by the employer to pay in future and by the employee to work in future provide the necessary consideration. Nevertheless, the contrary argument is not completely ruled out in the current state of UK law and there is therefore something to be said for ensuring that each side gives the other some benefit when there is any change in terms and conditions, so as to put this point beyond argument.

TERMINATION AND RE-EMPLOYMENT ON NEW TERMS

This is the only lawful alternative for any employer who has failed to achieve change by consent. As a matter of contract law an employer is free to bring contracts of employment to an end at any time by serving notice under the contract. Of course, such terminations would amount to dismissals for unfair dismissal purposes so attention must also be given to taking action to avoid findings being made that the dismissals are unfair. This is covered in more detail further on in this chapter.

So far as the contract of employment is concerned, typically the employer will, after exhausting negotiations, notify the employee in writing that the changes have not been implemented and give a period of time in order for acceptance. Sometimes a 'carrot' is offered in the form of a lump sum payment in return for acceptance within that time limit. It is made clear that if this final opportunity is not taken then the employer will have to proceed to terminate the existing contracts and offer re-employment on the new terms.

When the expiry date has been reached the employer then serves notice on all employees who have not agreed to the change to terminate their contracts of employment. Those notices can either be for the duration required by the individual contract of each particular employee or the employer may find it simpler to give notice to all employees of the length required for those employees with the longest notice entitlement. The letter of termination will confirm that re-employment, with full continuity of employment, is offered with immediate effect after the termination of the existing contract on the new, specified, terms. It will also state that any employee attending for work on or after the termination will be taken to have agreed to the new terms.

This procedure will be effective in putting all employees who attend work on the new terms. However, those employees have, in the process, been dismissed. The employees who have not accepted the new terms have of course also been dismissed. Both categories of employee can bring claims for unfair dismissal in the Industrial Tribunal, claims in which they are particularly likely to seek not only compensation but also reinstatement on the original terms of employment.

The onus is on the employer to establish that the reason for dismissal was a potentially fair one and the Tribunal must then decide whether in all the circumstances the employer acted reasonably in terminating the employment for that reason. The relevant potentially fair reason is the catch-all category of 'some other substantial reason'. The Tribunal will examine the reasons why the employer felt it necessary to make these changes. An absolute overwhelming necessity is not required, but the Tribunals will require a 'sound, good business reason' (*Hollister v National Farmers Union* (1979)[3]).

When it has found that the reason for the changes is substantial enough the Tribunal then have to weigh that reason against the impact on the individual employee. The Tribunal is not permitted to make its own judgment as to whether or not one set of interests outweighs the other – it must merely ask itself whether a reasonable employer, taking account, as such an employer would, of the impact of the changes on employees, could nevertheless reasonably come to the conclusion that the changes must be made (*Chubb Fire Securities Ltd v Harper* (1983)[4] and *Richmond Precision Engineering Ltd v Pearce* (1985)[5]). In assessing that general issue of reasonableness, the Tribunal will also look at how the employer went about making the changes in terms of negotiation and discussion and taking account of the circumstances of particular employees. For this reason it is prudent that all steps in the negotiations should be carefully documented.

There is an inconsistency here with the approach taken by Tribunals to redundancy situations. The case law authority (*James W Cook & Co (Wivenhoe) Ltd v Tipper* (1990)[6]) shows that it is no part of the function of the Industrial Tribunal to examine whether the employer had good reason to make the decision to reduce the number of employees, the Tribunal has to take that decision as read (provided that it is a genuine decision) and merely address whether or not a reasonable employer, having made the decision that reductions in numbers must be made, would insist on compulsory redundancy and would go about it in the way in which the particular employer had. Quite why it is that in the case of terminations to achieve change in terms and conditions the employer has to go further to show the sound, good business reasons is hard to understand – particularly since the impact on employees is much less serious than in redundancy – after all the employees will still have jobs at the end of the exercise. There is little doubt that the approach of the Tribunals in cases concerning changes in terms is hard to reconcile with the approach to redundancy cases. However, the leading cases on both sides were decided in the Court of Appeal and therefore employers should proceed on the basis that they will need to be able to prove a fairly convincing business case.

---

3   [1979] IRLR 2381.
4   [1983] IRLR 311.
5   [1985] IRLR 179.
6   [1990] IRLR 386.

UNILATERAL CHANGE

Some employers, when faced with a refusal by employees to consent to a change, simply impose it unilaterally. One particular attraction of this approach is that such action does not amount to a dismissal and accordingly if employees want to bring unfair dismissal claims the onus is on them to resign in order to claim constructive dismissal. Many employees will be reluctant to lose their jobs in return for the possibility of succeeding in a Tribunal claim. However, to balance that advantage from an employer's point of view, there are many disadvantages of unilateral action:

- the employer may not succeed in changing the contract;
- unions and employees may be provoked;
- the risk of unfair dismissal is higher;
- the risk of court injunctions.

We shall examine each of these points in turn:

The employer may not succeed in changing the contract. This will store up trouble for the future. For example, if a sick pay scheme is made less advantageous then an employee may carry on working and several years later, on falling sick, succeed in recovering the original sick pay benefits. In the case of *WPM Retail v Long* (1978)[7] an employee's bonus entitlement was changed adversely. He objected but carried on working and after three years successfully brought legal proceedings for the arrears of bonus.

In some cases the change in terms and conditions will be one where if the employee is to carry on working he or she will have to co-operate with the changes – for example, a change in working hours or in place of work. In such cases it is much more likely that after a period of time the Courts will hold that the employee has by conduct agreed to the new terms. Accordingly, for a change of this kind unilateral action is a more practical proposition, although even here there will be a 'reasonable' period of time before the employee will have to elect whether to accept the new terms or resign and claim constructive dismissal.

Unions and employees may be provoked. Unilateral action will be seen as more high-handed by employees and unions and accordingly the level of dispute and the number of Tribunal claims is likely to be higher than if proper notice of termination is given.

The risk of unfair dismissal is higher. Unilateral change is an inherently unlawful way of proceeding and is consequently harder to justify as

---

7   [1978] IRLR 243.

reasonable. Accordingly the employer may well lose claims for unfair dismissal even in cases where there are good and substantial reasons for the change.

The risk of court injunctions. Since the employer is acting in breach of contract, employees may apply to the courts for a declaration as to the terms of the contract or even for an injunction. A court decision adverse to the employer will be a serious setback to the process of change.

CHANGE PURSUANT TO CONTRACTUAL RIGHTS

Many contracts have some degree of flexibility written into them. For example, a contract of employment may state that the employee is employed at 'X hospital or such other location within the geographical area served by the Trust as is specified by the Trust from time to time'. Such a provision does give the employer a right to change the employee's place of work, although any such power must be exercised in a reasonable way which enables the employee to comply (the *United Bank Ltd v Akhtar* (1989)[8] and *White v Reflecting Roadstuds Ltd* (1981)[9]).

At the other extreme, a contract which says 'You will work for the Trust in such place, carrying out such duties, for such pay, as the Trust may from time to time specify', is unlikely to be held by the courts to be a contract at all since it is too uncertain.

The courts, sensibly, are cautious about flexibility clauses since they can enable the party possessing the flexibility to behave oppressively. Accordingly, where an employer requires flexibility it should make that power as clear and precise as possible. If a particular clause of this kind can be interpreted broadly or narrowly the court is likely to opt for the narrower interpretation. For example, if the employee's hours of work is stated to be 'rotas as specified by the employer from time to time', a court is likely to interpret that as meaning that the employee can be given any rota within the existing pattern of shifts and rotas, and not as meaning that shifts and rotas can be changed completely.

The courts are less vigilant if the changes under a flexibility term are determined by a third party rather than unilaterally by the employer – for example if a contract provides for payment to be at a rate determined by some third party, or by negotiation between the employer's association and the unions, then that will almost certainly be given full effect by the courts.

In essence the situation here is one of shades of grey rather than black and white. The prudent advice to the employer who wishes to keep out of court, is

---

[8]   [1989] IRLR 507.
[9]   [1981] IRLR 331.

to use flexibility clauses only to achieve changes for individuals rather than for the workforce as a whole, and to ensure that the changes are either typical ones that occur quite commonly within the organisation or ones that do not make major alterations to the realities of the employee's working life. Of course, an employer may wish to use a flexibility clause as part of the negotiating stance for achieving more substantial changes, but it would be imprudent to rely upon the clause alone.

CHAPTER 11

IDEAS FOR LOCALLY NEGOTIATED TERMS OF EMPLOYMENT

INTRODUCTION

Many Trusts are using their independence in order to devise new sets of terms and conditions of employment that more accurately reflect their requirements and which are simpler to operate and to re-negotiate. The advent of the internal market and the competitive pressures which that brings mean that many terms of employment which were previously inappropriate in the health service, but common in the private sector, must now be given serious consideration by NHS Trusts and indeed by purchaser authorities.

In this chapter the authors examine a number of possible changes that health service managers should consider if they are seeking to negotiate their own locally agreed terms. Inevitably, this chapter is a mixture of law and the personal opinions of the authors.

SIMPLICITY

The complexity of traditional health service terms of employment and the advantages and disadvantages that this entails were discussed above. For many employers an attraction of locally negotiated terms will be the opportunity to introduce significantly simpler schemes. For many simplicity will not be a mere advantage but a necessity since individual negotiation with the current myriad of unions and bargaining groups would absorb far too much time. All the following are possibilities:

- a reduction in the number of different pay groups and bargaining groups;

- a reduction in the number of bands or steps in salary scales;

- simpler and fewer allowances and expense payments;

- simpler rules on matters such as annual leave and sick pay entitlement.

INCENTIVISATION

There are limited elements of performance related pay within the health service. The two most obvious examples are the system for general managers and the merit award system for consultants. NHS Trusts may consider it appropriate to introduce additional or alternative performance related pay schemes. The appropriateness of such schemes, and indeed their operability, varies tremendously from one occupational group to another within the health service. Doctors, for example, would argue that whilst the number of patients seen or the waiting time for an appointment can be measured, the most important aspects of their performance are not measurable.

For all its difficulties, the advocates of performance related pay would say that it harnesses the natural instincts of most people to try to earn more money, rewards those who work hard whilst minimising rewards for the lazy and ineffective, and offers the opportunity for increases in pay over and above inflation.

From the legal point of view, any performance related pay scheme must be carefully and coherently written so that the rules are understandable and workable. Most performance related pay schemes will involve an element of discretion or subjective assessment and it is vital that these elements are carefully designed and that they are operated properly in practice. There is a particular danger of discrimination on grounds of sex or race and employers as sophisticated as NHS Trusts would be expected by Industrial Tribunals to include monitoring procedures to uncover both deliberate favouritism and unconscious bias on sex or race grounds – or indeed just on grounds of personal likes and dislikes.

JOB EVALUATION

Many Trusts are looking afresh at the value put on the jobs of their employees. In many cases this is part of an overall drive towards a greater simplicity of pay and managerial structures but there is also an impetus for this work that derives from the law on equal pay. A woman can compare her pay and other terms and conditions in law with any man employed by the same employer if her work is of equal value to his. The case of *Enderby v Frenchay Health Authority* (1994)[1], demonstrates this comparison can be made from one professional group across to an entirely different one. There is a real danger that this principle will lead to a leapfrogging of pay claims and entitlements. This general topic is covered in more detail later in this chapter. One practical step that employers can take to minimise equal pay claims, and in some cases

---

[1]   [1994] IRLR 112, ECJ.

to prevent them, is to introduce proper job evaluation schemes and then to fix salaries and wages according to the results of such schemes. A proper job evaluation scheme provides a *prima facie* defence to an equal pay claim.

CONTRACTUAL FLEXIBILITY

The practical operation of flexibility clauses is examined in Chapter 10. Any employer reviewing terms and conditions of employment should think about what flexibilities it needs to write in. Typically, these will cover geographical mobility and job flexibility and they may also apply to hours of work, times of work and acting up.

Flexibility clauses have an impact not only upon what employees can be required to do – and indeed expect to be required to do – but also upon redundancy. If the degree of flexibility in the contract is low then a reduction in demand for a particular type of employee is likely to lead to redundancy, whereas if there is a considerable amount of flexibility in the contract, then there may be no redundancy at all since the employee can be transferred to other work. The law on this topic is currently in a state of flux as a result of established case law having been thrown into doubt by the case of *Bass Leisure Ltd v Thomas* (1994)[2] but the fact remains that the more flexible the contract, the less likely it is that a Tribunal will find, in a particular case, that there is a redundancy situation. That may be to the advantage or the disadvantage of the employer depending upon the circumstances.

PROTECTION AGAINST COMPETITION

This is a very new topic in the health service and directly results from the introduction of the internal market. The interests of an individual Trust or an individual purchaser could be seriously affected by the actions of employees or former employees. In the private sector it would be normal for employees who are in possession of confidential information that could assist the competition, and also employees who have vested in them personally the goodwill of their employer, to be subject to contractual restrictions on their activities both during their employment and after their employment has come to an end.

So far as protecting confidential information during employment is concerned, even in the health service there are implied obligations. However, most health service employees are entirely free to join any other employer

---

[2] [1994] IRLR 104.

after they have left their existing employer. It is easy to imagine circumstances in which an employee moving from one provider to another or from a provider to a purchaser, could do significant harm to the financial interests of the former employer in the course of seeking to advance the interests of the new employer.

For those reasons health service employers should carefully consider imposing express restrictions on confidential information worded to continue to apply after termination of the employment. There is considerable legal doubt at the moment about the extent to which express confidentiality clauses can go beyond what is implied, but there is no doubt that the former employer's case is assisted if it has spelt out that certain categories of information are confidential and has required the employee not to disclose or make use of them to others except insofar as that knowledge is inextricably bound up in the employee's own professional skill and competence.

The other standard contractual measure taken to deal with this problem is the imposition of what are known as restrictive covenants. These are restrictions upon the work and business activities that the employee can undertake for a limited period of time after termination of employment. Since such clauses interfere with the free market and reduce individuals' ability to earn a living, the courts police them carefully and will enforce them only insofar as they are necessary to protect the legitimate interests of the former employer and are reasonable in the interests of the public as a whole.

So far as the authors are aware, there has been no decided case on restrictive covenants in the health service or any similar service. However, as a matter of general principle the advent of the internal market clearly creates sources of income that former employers have a legitimate interest to protect and, given the government policy that a market system in the health service will work to the benefit of the public, there is no reason in legal public policy why the competitive entities within the internal market should not be able to protect themselves against the abuse of confidential information or goodwill. For that reason the authors have advised NHS Trusts who are reviewing their terms and conditions, particularly at senior levels such as executive directors, to consider the introduction of restrictive covenants. Typically, a Trust director might be barred from working for a period of one year for any purchaser with whom the provider had a contract or for any provider acting, or seeking to act, in competition with the employer.

Because of the courts' concern to minimise restraints of this kind, such clauses need to be very carefully worded and need to be adapted to the particular circumstances of each employee or category of employees. It is most definitely a job for lawyers.

UNION DE-RECOGNITION

There is no legal obligation on any employer to recognise any Trade Union, although in cases of collective dismissals for redundancy or other reasons there are obligations under UK law and European law to consult with representatives of workers. Employers are therefore free to refuse to recognise or de-recognise trade unions. In the NHS it is unlikely that any Trust would wish to de-recognise altogether, but some Trusts have sought to reduce the number of unions with whom they negotiate. Are there any legal risks in taking such action?

The only legal risk relates to the right of any employee to seek the protection of the Industrial Tribunal if he or she is dismissed or subjected to any other detriment for Trade Union membership, or for taking part in the activities of a Trade Union at an appropriate time, or for Trade Union non-membership (sections 146 and 152 of the Trade Union and Labour Relations (Consolidation) Act 1992). This protection applies whether or not the union is recognised by the employer.

In the recognition context, what sometimes occurs is that the employer seeks to agree individual contracts with employees to replace collectively negotiated ones. Inevitably, such individual contracts are likely to contain improvements over the existing collectively negotiated terms and the argument therefore has been that those employees who do not accept individual contracts are being deprived of the improvements and thus subjected to a detriment for Trade Union membership or activities.

In the cases of *Wilson v Associated Newspaper Ltd* and *Palmer v Associated British Parks* (1993)[3] the Court of Appeal held in 1993 that such action was indeed the unlawful imposition of detriment on Trade Union grounds. However, this was reversed by an amendment to section 148 of the Trade Union and Labour Relations (Consolidation) Act 1992 implemented by the Trade Union Reform and Employment Rights Act 1993. In 1995 the House of Lords also overturned the Court of Appeal decision. The combined result is as follows:

1 It is not unlawful to take action which has the indirect consequence of deterring union membership such as action to encourage employees to abandon collective bargaining. It appears that this even avoids the special protection against dismissal on union grounds.

2 'Omissions' rather than 'actions' on the part of the employer are lawful even if the direct purpose is to penalise employees for union membership or activities – this would include not awarding pay rises to union members.

---

[3] [1993] IRLR 336.

3   It is not unlawful to impose detriments on employees for Trade Union membership or activities if one of the purposes of the employer in creating those detriments was to achieve a change in its relationship with all its employees or any class of employee. Accordingly, an employer who wishes to change from collective negotiation with a union to individual negotiation with employees can claim the protection of this section. However, there is a proviso that the protection only applies if the action is action which a reasonable employer could take.

Points 1 and 2 stem from the House of Lords decision and are startling. Tribunals will be uncomfortable with them and it would be a brave employer who relied on point 1 to go so far as to dismiss individual employees who refused to sign individual contracts. If such employees succeeded in the Tribunal they would be entitled to very substantial levels of compensation.

Overall, the current state of the law is such that if an employer is seeking to reduce or eliminate Trade Union recognition or to cut trade unions out of the contractual bargaining process to any extent, then legal advice should be taken in order to ensure that the law protecting employees Trade Union activities is not inadvertently broken.

INDEX

Absenteeism, 12
  dismissals for, 112-113
  incompetence and, 112
  misconduct as, 112
  monitoring, 112
  procedure on, 112
  sick pay and, 12
Acquired Rights Directive, 79-102
  See also TRANSFER OF
  UNDERTAKINGS
  compensation and, 107
  direct effect of, 80
  health service and, 79-81
  interpretation of, 81
  revision of, 86-87, 102
  unfair dismissal and, 107
Acting-up
  locally negotiated contracts and, 149
  terms and conditions of
    employment and, 1, 149
  written conditions of
    employment and, 6
Advertising
  Commission of Racial Equality and, 44
  discrimination and, 43-44
  Equal Opportunities
    Commission and, 44
Allowances
  maternity rights and, 23
  protection of earnings and, 16
  written particulars of
    employment and, 6
Ante natal care, 26

Benefits, 52, 137
Bonus schemes, 101

Codes of practice
  ACAS, 108
  Commission of Racial
    Equality and, 43, 45
  disabled persons and, 61
  disciplinary procedures and, 108
  Equal Opportunities
    Commission and, 39, 43, 50
  homosexuality on, 57
Collective agreements
  equal pay and, 72-73, 77
  trade union recognition and, 151
  transfer of undertakings and, 80

written particulars of
  employment and, 4, 5
Commission for Racial Equality, 39
  advertising and, 44
  codes of practice and, 43, 45
  interviewing and, 46
Compensation
  Acquired Rights Directive and, 107
  benefits for, 137
  breaches of contract and, 135-137
  disciplinary procedures and, 8
  discrimination and, 63-64
  dismissals for, 152
  equal pay and, 66
  fixed term contracts and, 126, 135
  guidance on, 135, 137
  injuries to feelings and, 64
  interest on, 64
  locally negotiated contracts and, 152
  maternity rights and, 63-64
  measure of loss and, 135-137
  notice and, 136
  payments in lieu of notice and, 136-137
  ready reckoners and, 138
  re-employment and, 142
  superannuation and, 138
  taxation and, 136-138
  transfer of undertakings and, 96
  unfair dismissal for, 107
Confidentiality, 17-20, 110-111
  competition and, 19
  disclosure and, 18-19
  dismissals and, 110-111
  employers' affairs and, 19-20
  exceptions to, 18
  guidance on, 18
  harassment and, 111
  Industrial Tribunals in, 111-112
  locally negotiated
    contracts and, 149-150
  patients and, 17-19
  public interest and, 18-19, 20
  terms and conditions of
    employment and, 17-20, 149-150
  Whitley Councils and, 17-20
Consultants
  discipline of, 115-129
  dismissal of, 115-129
  incompetence of, 116-117
  mental health and, 117
  misconduct by, 116-117
  physical disabilities of, 117

Consultation
  dismissals on, 113-114
  redundancies and, 99, 151
  transfer of undertakings and, 81, 88, 89, 91-96, 99
  trade unions with, 81, 88, 89, 92, 113-114
Continuity of employment
  maternity rights and, 21-22, 23, 28
  redundancy payments and, 12, 13-14, 107
  re-employment and, 142
  terms and conditions of employment and, 12-13
  transfers of undertaking and, 12-13
  unfair dismissal and, 107
  Whitley Councils and, 12-13
  written particulars of employment and, 3, 5
Contracting out
  contract of employment and, 132, 133-134
  equal pay legislation of, 76
  fixed term contracts and, 133
  pension schemes and, 4
  redundancies and, 132, 134
  transfer of undertakings and, 79, 87, 92, 97
  unfair dismissal and, 132-134
  written particulars of employment and, 4
Contracts of employment
  breach of, 134-135
  contracting out and, 132, 133-134
  equal pay and, 74-75
  event, 132-134
  fixed term, 132-134
  minimum term, 132
  notice and, 131
  protection of employment and, 17
  purpose, 132-134
  redundancy and, 132, 134-135
  resignation and, 135
  short term rolling, 132
  termination of, 134-135
  transfer of undertakings and, 96-102
  unfair dismissal and, 132-134
  written particulars of employment and, 7-9
Crime
  disclosure and, 19
  transfer of undertakings and, 98

Damages.
See COMPENSATION
Deductions
  itemised pay statements and, 10
  written particulars of employment and, 9
Defences
  disabled persons and, 59
  discrimination and, 42-43, 59-60, 62
  equal pay and, 71-74
  racial discrimination and, 42
Department of Health
  guidance on confidentiality (draft) and, 18
Disabled persons
  codes of practice and, 61
  defences and, 59
  definition of, 58-59
  discrimination and, 58-61
  dismissals and, 58, 61
  ill health and, 60
  policies on, 61
  promotion and, 58
  quotas and, 60
  recruitment and, 58, 61
  register of, 60
  trade unions and, 61
  training and, 58, 59
  transfers and, 58
  unfair dismissal and, 60
  Whitley Council and, 58
Disciplinary procedures
  ACAS Code of Practice and, 108
  appeals and, 119-120, 124
    Secretary of State to, 127-129
  assessments and, 122-124
  breach of, 8-9, 135
  compensation and, 8-9
  consultants and, 115-129
  delay in, 109-110
  Department of Health Circular HC (90) (9) and, 116
  dismissals and, 108, 115-129
  doctors and, 116-129
  enquires and, 125-127
  HC (90) (9) Annex B procedure and, 116
  health service in, 108, 115
  injunctions and, 8-9
  Intermediate Procedure and, 116-117, 122
  Professional Review Machinery and, 116-117, 120-124

remuneration and, 129
Serious Disciplinary
    Procedure and, 117
serious misconduct or
    incompetence and, 124-127
suspension and, 124
three wise men procedure and, 117
trade unions and, 108
written particulars of
    employment and, 4, 5, 8-9
Disclosure
confidentiality and, 18-19
crime and, 19
public interest in, 18-19
Discrimination, 39-64
See also COMMISSION FOR
RACIAL EQUALITY,
EQUAL OPPORTUNITIES
COMMISSION, EQUAL PAY,
HOMOSEXUALITY, RACIAL
DISCRIMINATION, SEX
DISCRIMINATION
advertising and, 43-45
age, 40
application forms and, 45
benefits and, 52
'but for' test and, 41-42, 57
capability and, 60
compensation and, 63-64
constructive dismissal and, 53-54, 144
course of employment and, 42, 62
defences to, 42-43, 59-60, 62
definition of, 59
direct, 40, 45-46, 61
disabled persons and, 58-61
dismissal and, 50, 53, 58, 61
employers' liability and, 42-43
European Union and, 40, 52, 55, 57, 61
facilities and, 52
genuine occupational
    circumstances and, 46-49
harassment and, 53, 61-64
homosexuality and, 40, 56-57
ill health and, 60
indirect, 40-41, 46, 50, 51, 53
injuries to feelings awards and, 64
interviews and, 46
job sharing and, 52
married persons and, 40, 49
maternity rights and, 26, 29, 30-31,
    36, 52, 63
mobility clauses and, 52-53
newsletters and, 44

part-time workers and, 53, 55-56
policy on, 43
positive, 44
performance-related pay and, 148
pre-employment and, 43-49
proceedings and, 63-64
promotion and, 50-51, 58
questionnaire and, 62-63
quotas and, 60-61
'reasonable practicable' and, 42-43, 62
recruitment and, 43, 45, 58
redundancies and, 53, 55
remedies and, 62-64
selection and, 58
self-employed workers and, 39
shortlisting and, 45-46
sick pay and, 52
stereotyping and, 45, 46
trade unions and, 45, 52
training and, 50, 51-52, 58, 59
transfers and, 50-51, 58
transsexuals and, 57
unfair dismissal and, 60, 107
vicarious liability and, 42-43, 62
victimisation and, 54-55
Whitley Council and, 29, 57, 61
Dismissals, 105-114
See also REDUNDANCIES,
UNFAIR DISMISSAL
absenteeism and, 112-113
ACAS Code of Practice and, 108
appeals against, 117
changes in terms and conditions
    of employment and, 140, 144
compensation on, 113-114
confidentiality and, 110-111
constructive, 53-54, 144
consultation and, 113-114
consultants and, 115-129
decisions on, 126-127
defamation and, 121
delay and, 109-110
disabled persons and, 61
disciplinary procedures and, 108,
    115-129
discrimination and, 50, 53, 58, 61
fairness of, 105-106, 142
fixed term contracts and, 133
harassment and, 53
health service and, 108-112
ill-health for, 12, 112-113
maternity rights and, 28-32
misbehaviour and, 112

procedure for, 106-107, 108-112
publicity and, 110-112
reasonableness of, 106-107, 143
re-employment and, 144
sexual misconduct for, 111
summary, 110
suspension and, 110
terms and conditions of
employment and, 140
trade unions and, 108, 113-114,
51-152
transfer of undertakings and, 81, 97-98,
101, 102
under-performance and, 108-109, 112
Whitley Committees and, 108
wrongful, 135
Doctors.
See CONSULTANTS

Equal opportunities.
See COMMISSION FOR RACIAL
EQUALITY, DISCRIMINATION,
EQUAL OPPORTUNITIES
COMMISSION, EQUAL PAY, SEX
DISCRIMINATION
Equal Opportunities Commission
advertising and, 44
aims of, 39
codes of practice by, 39, 43, 50
harassment and, 61-62
interviewing and, 46
Sexual Harassment – What Can
You Do About It?, 61-62
Equal pay, 65-77
audits, 76
claims for, 70-72, 75-77
collective bargaining and, 72-73, 77
comparators and, 68-70, 74
compensation and, 66
contracting out of legislation and, 76
contracts of employment and, 74-75
defences and, 71-74
definition of 'pay' and, 67-68
Directive on, 65, 75
equal value and, 66, 73-74
European Union and, 65-68, 73, 77
experts and, 73-74
job evaluation studies and, 73, 77,
148-149
material factors and, 71-74
objectively justified factors and, 72
occupational pensions and, 68

part-time workers and, 68
prevention of claims and, 76-77
time limits and, 75
trade unions and, 72-73
Equal Treatment Directive, 57
European Union
changes in terms and conditions
of employment and, 140
discrimination and, 40, 52, 55, 57, 61
equal pay and, 65-68, 73, 77
harassment and, 61
homosexuality and, 57
maternity rights and, 21, 30, 33
part-time workers and, 55
terms and conditions of
employment and, 140

Fixed term contracts, 132-134
compensation and, 126, 135
contracting out and, 133
dismissals and, 133
maternity rights and, 31-32
notice and, 132, 134

Genuine occupational
qualifications, 46-49
Group of companies, 90

Harassment
confidentiality and, 111
discrimination and, 53, 61-62
dismissal and, 53
Equal Opportunities
Commission and, 61-62
European Commission's
Code of Practice and, 61
vicarious liability and, 62
Health and safety
maternity rights and, 32-36
unfair dismissals and, 107
Health and Safety Executive Guide for
Employers. New and Expectant
Mothers at Work, 32-33
Health service
Acquired Rights Directive and, 79-81
appeals procedure in the, 109
disciplinary procedures and, 108, 115
dismissals and, 108-114
management and, 108-109
pensions and, 114
redundancies in, 114

under-performance in, 108-109, 112
warnings and, 109
Holidays
maternity rights and, 23, 25, 26
negotiated terms of
employment and, 147
protection of earnings and, 16
remuneration and, 16
terms and conditions of
employment and, 1, 16, 147
written particulars of
employment and, 4, 5, 6
Homosexuality
'but for' test and, 57
codes of practice and, 57
discrimination and, 40, 56-57
equal treatment and, 57
European Union and, 57
sex discrimination and, 57
transsexuals and, 57
unfair dismissal and, 57
Whitley Council and, 57
Hours of work
changes in terms and conditions
of employment and, 145
locally negotiated contracts and, 149
reduction in, 16
remuneration and, 16
terms and conditions of
employment and, 145, 149
written particulars of
employment and, 4, 5

Ill health,
See also ABSENTEEISM, SICK LEAVE,
SICK PAY
alternative employment and, 113
disabled persons and, 60
discrimination and, 60
dismissal for, 12, 112-113
early retirement and, 15
maternity leave and, 24
medical advice and, 113
retirement and, 113
superannuation and, 114
sick pay and, 12
Whitley Councils and, 112
Incompetence
absenteeism and, 112
appeals to Secretary of
State and, 127-129
consultants and, 116-120
definitions of, 119

disciplinary procedure and, 124-127
Whitley Councils and, 119
Indemnities, 89
Industrial Tribunals
confidentiality in, 111-112
written particulars of
employment and, 6
Information
confidentiality and, 17-20, 110-111
locally negotiated
contracts and, 149-150
patients and, 17-19
transfer of undertakings and, 81, 89,
91, 92-96
written particulars of
employment in, 3-6
Injunctions
changes in terms and conditions
of employment and, 145
disciplinary procedures and, 8-9
written particulars of
employment and, 8
Interviews, 46
Itemised pay statements, 8-9, 10

Job descriptions, 4, 5
Job evaluation, 148-149
Job sharing, 26, 52
Job titles, 4, 5

Locally-negotiated contracts
acting-up and, 149
compensation and, 152
confidentiality and, 149-150
hours of work and, 149
information and, 149-150
mobility and, 149
redundancies and, 149
restrictive covenants and, 150
sick pay and, 147
terms and conditions of
employment and, 147-152
trade unions and, 151-152

Market testing, 79, 87, 88
Married persons, 40, 49
Maternity rights, 21-37
allowances and, 23
alternative employment and, 26-27,
32-33, 35-36

ante-natal care and, 26
compensation and, 63-64
compulsory, 25
contractual, 21
continuity of employment and, 21-22, 23, 28
discrimination and, 28, 29, 30-31, 36, 52
dismissal and, 23, 27, 28-32, 63
enforcement of, 28
European Union and, 21, 30, 33
extended, 21
fixed term contracts and, 31-32
guidance on, 32-35
health and safety and, 32-36
holiday leave and, 23, 25, 26
ill-health and, 24
job sharing and, 26
locally-negotiated contracts and, 63-64
loss of, 29-30
night workers and, 33
notice and, 23-24, 25, 29-30
part-time employees and, 21, 23, 26, 36
pensions and, 23
policy on, 26
Pregnant Workers Directive and, 21, 31, 33
redundancy and, 27
remuneration and, 23, 25, 31, 36-37
return to work and, 23, 24, 25, 26-30, 36-37
risk assessment and, 32
sick leave and, 31
sick pay and, 21, 24, 31
statutory, 21-23, 24, 25-26, 36-37
suspension and, 32-33, 35-36
terms and conditions of
    employment and, 1, 23, 25
time limits and, 29
training and, 31
unfair dismissal and, 23, 27, 28-30
Whitley Councils and, 21-22, 23-26, 31-32, 36-37

Media, 17-20

Misconduct
    absenteeism and, 112
    appeals to Secretary of State on, 127-129
    consultants and, 116-120
    definition of, 118-119
    disciplinary procedures and, 124-127
    investigations and, 125-126
    serious, 124-127
    sexual, 111

summary dismissal for, 135
suspension for, 124
time limits and, 124-125
Whitley Councils and, 119

Mobility
    discrimination and, 52-53
    locally negotiated contracts and, 149
    terms and conditions of
        employment and, 1, 149
    transfer of undertakings and, 90
    written particulars of
        employment and, 7

National Health Service Management
Executive. Guidance for Staff on
Relations with the Public and the
Media June 1993, 19, 20

Night work, 33

Notice
    breach of contract and, 134
    compensation and, 136
    contract of employment and, 131
    fixed term contracts and, 132, 134
    maternity rights and, 23-24, 25-29, 30
    payment in lieu of, 136-138
    protection of earnings and, 16
    re-employment and, 142
    remuneration and, 16
    terms and conditions of
        employment and, 16, 139
    written particulars of
        employment and, 4, 5-6

Overtime, 16

Part-time workers
    discrimination and, 53, 55-56
    equal pay and, 68
    European Union and, 55
    maternity rights and, 21, 23, 26, 36
    redundancy and, 55
    Payments in lieu of notice, 136-138

Pensions schemes
    contracting out and, 4
    early retirement and, 14, 15, 114
    equal pay and, 68
    health service and, 114
    maternity leave and, 23
    misconduct of, 124
    retirement and, 15

terms and conditions of
employment and, 15
transfer of undertakings and, 81, 98,
99-100
Whitley Councils and, 114
written particulars of
employment and, 4, 5
Performance-related pay, 148
Pregnancy.
See MATERNITY RIGHTS
Pregnant Workers Directive, 21, 31, 33
Profit sharing, 101
Promotion
disabled persons and, 58
discrimination and, 50-51, 58
Public interest, 18-19, 20

Racial discrimination.
See also COMMISSION FOR RACIAL
EQUALITY, DISCRIMINATION
'but for' test and, 41-42
defences and, 42
direct, 40
genuine occupational
qualifications and, 46, 49
indirect, 41
vicarious liability and, 42-43
Recruitment
disabilities and, 58, 61
discrimination and, 43, 45, 58
Redundancies
alternative employment and, 13-14, 17
calculation of service and, 13-14
consultation on, 99, 151
continuity of employment and, 12,
13-14, 107
contract of employment and, 132,
134-135
contracting out and, 132, 134
discrimination and, 53, 55
flexibility clauses and, 149
health service in, 114
locally negotiated contracts and, 149
maternity leave and, 27
part-timers and, 55
protection of earnings and, 14, 17
retirement and, 14
terms and conditions of
employment and, 1, 12, 13-14
transfer of undertakings and, 99
Whitley Councils and, 12, 13-14

Re-employment
compensation and, 142
continuity of employment and, 142
dismissals and, 144
new terms on, 142-143
notice and, 142
terms and conditions of
employment and, 142-145
Reengagement, 107
Reinstatement, 107, 109, 142
Remuneration,
See also EQUAL PAY
agreements on, 16
allowances and, 16
contract of employment and, 17
deductions and, 9-10
disciplinary proceedings and, 129
downgrading and, 16
holidays and, 16
hours of work and, 16
itemised pay statements and, 9-10
maternity rights and, 23, 25, 31, 36-37
notice periods and, 16
overtime and, 16
payments in lieu of notice and, 136-138
performance-related pay and, 148
protection of, 16-17
reorganisations and, 17
subsidence and, 16
redundancies and, 17
terms and conditions of
employment and, 16-17
travel and, 16
transfer of employment and, 16, 17
Whitley Council and, 16-17
written particulars of
employment and, 3, 5, 9
Reorganisations, 17
Resignation, 135
Restrictive covenants
locally negotiated contracts and, 150
transfer of undertakings and, 100
Retirement
early, 14, 15, 114
ill-health for, 113
pensions and, 15
protection of pay and, 14
redundancies and, 14
superannuation and, 15
terms and conditions of
employment and, 14, 15
Whitley Councils and, 15

Self-employed persons, 39

Sex discrimination,
  See also DISCRIMINATION, EQUAL
  OPPORTUNITIES COMMISSION,
  EQUAL PAY, HARASSMENT
  application forms and, 45
  'but for' test and, 41-42
  direct, 40
  genuine occupational
    qualifications and, 46-49
  homosexuality and, 57
  indirect, 40-41
  maternity leave and, 28, 29, 30-31,
    36, 52
  part-time workers and, 53, 55-56
  written particulars of
    employment and, 6

Share option schemes, 101

Sick leave,
  See also SICK PAY
  maternity rights and, 31
  terms and conditions of
    employment and, 1
  written particulars of
    employment and, 5

Sick pay,
  See also SICK LEAVE
  absenteeism and, 12
  calculation of, 11-12
  discrimination and, 52
  dismissals for ill-health and, 12
  exhaustion of, 113
  locally negotiated terms of
    employment and, 147
  maternity rights and, 21, 24, 31
  statutory, 12
  terms and conditions of
    employment and, 1, 11-12, 147
  Whitley Council and, 11-12, 112, 113
  written particulars of
    employment and, 4, 5

Sickness.
  See ILL-HEALTH

Shortlisting, 45-46

Superannuation
  compensation and, 138
  early retirement and, 15, 114
  ill health and, 114
  compensation ready reckoner and, 138

Suspension
  disciplinary procedures and, 124
  dismissals and, 110

maternity rights and, 32-33, 35-36
misconduct and, 124

Taxation, 136-138

Tenders, 83, 89, 92, 93, 97

Terms and conditions of
  employment, 1-10
  See also WRITTEN PARTICULARS
  OF EMPLOYMENT
  acting-up and, 1, 149
  central bargaining and, 1-2
  changes to, 7, 17, 139-146
  conduct and, 144
  consent to, 139-142
  dismissals and, 140
  European Union and, 140
  injunctions and, 145
  notice of, 139
  re-employment and, 142-145
  trade unions and, 139-140, 144
  unfair dismissal and, 144-145
  unilateral and, 144-145
  collective negotiated, 151
  comparisons between, 148
  confidentiality and, 17-20, 149-150
  continuity of employment and, 12-13
  contractual rights and, 1
  determination of, 1
  flexibility in, 2, 145-146, 149
  holidays and, 1, 16, 147
  hours of work and, 145, 149
  inflexibility in, 2
  job evaluation and, 148-149
  locally negotiated, 147-152
  maternity rights and, 1, 23, 25
  media and, 17-20
  mobility and, 1, 149
  nationwide, 1
  negotiation and, 1-2
  notice and, 16
  pensions and, 15
  performance-related pay and, 148
  redundancy payments and, 1, 12, 13-14
  re-employment on new
    terms and, 142-145
  remuneration and, 16-17
  restrictive covenants and, 150
  retirement and, 14, 15
  Review Bodies on, 1
  sick leave and, 1
  sick pay and, 1, 11-12, 147
  special health service terms and, 11-20
  subsidence and, 16

trade union recognition
  agreements and, 2
transfers of undertaking and, 12-13, 16, 101-102
travel and, 16
trusts and, 2-3
Whitley Councils and, 1-2, 11-20
workplaces and, 145
Time limits
  equal pay and, 75
  maternity rights and, 29
  misconduct and, 124-125
  written particulars of
    employment and, 3
Trade unions
  changes in terms and conditions of
    employment and, 139, 140, 144
  collective negotiations and, 151
  consultation with, 81, 88, 89, 92, 113-114
  disabled persons and, 61
  disciplinary procedures and, 108
  discrimination and, 45, 52
  dismissals and, 108, 113-114, 151-152
  equal pay and, 72-73
  locally negotiated
    contracts and, 151-152
  recognition of, 2, 81, 113, 151-152
  representation, 113
  terms and conditions of
    employment and, 12-13, 16, 101-102
  transfer of undertakings and, 79, 80, 88, 89, 92-96, 99
  unfair dismissal and, 107
Training
  disabled persons and, 58, 59
  discrimination and, 50, 51-52, 58, 59
  equal opportunities and, 62
  maternity leave and, 31
Transfer of undertakings, 79-103
  See also ACQUIRED
  RIGHTS DIRECTIVES
  bonus schemes and, 101
  collective agreements and, 80
  compensation and, 96
  consultation and, 81, 88-89, 91-96, 99
  continuity of employment and, 12-13
  contracting out and, 79, 87, 92, 97
  contracts of employment and, 96-102
  criminal liabilities and, 98
  disabled persons and, 58
  discrimination and, 50-51, 58
  dismissals and, 81, 97-98, 101, 102

employees and, 88-91
  assignment of, 89-90
  objections to, 103
European Union and, 79-103
groups of companies and, 90
health sector and, 79-80, 84-85, 91
indemnities and, 89
information and, 81, 88-89, 91, 92-96
liabilities and, 102
market testing and, 79, 87, 88
mobility clauses and, 90
negligence claims and, 99
pensions and, 81, 98, 99-100
profit sharing and, 101
protection of earnings and, 16, 17
redundancies and, 99
remuneration and, 16, 17
restrictive covenants and, 100
share option clauses and, 101
tenders and, 83, 89, 92, 93, 97
terms and conditions of
  employment and, 101-102
trade unions and, 79, 80-81, 88, 89, 92-96, 99
'transfers' and, 81, 84-87
trusts and, 91
'undertakings' and, 81-84
unfair dismissal and, 81, 97-98, 107
Whitley Council and, 12-13
Transsexuals, 57

Unfair dismissal, 105-114
  Acquired Rights Directive and, 107
  changes in terms and conditions of
    employment and, 144-145
  compensation for, 107
  continuity of employment and, 107
  contracting out and, 132-134
  contracts of employment and, 132-134
  discrimination and, 60, 107
  disabled persons and, 60
  health and safety and, 107
  health service and, 105-114
  homosexuality and, 57
  maternity leave and, 23, 27, 28-30
  re-engagement and, 107
  reinstatement and, 107
  remedies for, 107
  trade unions and, 107
  transfer of undertakings and, 81, 97-98, 107
written particulars of
  employment and, 6

Vicarious liability
    discrimination and,   42-43, 62
    harassment and,   62
Victimisation,   54-55

Wages.
    See HOLIDAY PAY,
    REMUNERATION
Whitley Councils
    advantages of,   1
    confidentiality and,   17-20
    continuity of employment and,   12-13
    disabled persons and,   58
    discrimination and,   39, 57-61
    dismissals and,   108
    homosexuality and,   57
    ill-health for,   112
    incompetence and,   119
    maternity rights and,   21-22, 23-26,
                    31-32, 26-37
    misconduct and,   119
    pension schemes and,   114
    protection of earnings and,   16-17
    redundancies and,   12, 13-14
    retirement and,   15
    sick pay and,   11-12, 112-113
    terms and conditions of
      employment and,   1-2, 11-20
    transfer of undertakings and,   12-13
    written conditions of
      employment and,   6
Working abroad,   4
Working rules,   9, 145
Workplaces,   4, 5
Written particulars of employment,   3-9
    See also TERMS AND CONDITIONS
    OF EMPLOYMENT
    acting-up rules and,   6
    allowances and,   6
    changes to,   7
    collective agreements and,   4, 5
    continuity of employment and,   3, 5
    contracting out and,   4
    contracts of employment and,   7-9
    cross-references to other
      documents and,   3, 5-6
    deductions and,   9
    demotion and,   7
    disciplinary rules and,   4, 5, 8-9
    employment abroad and,   4
    grievance procedure and,   4, 5, 8
    holidays and,   4, 5, 6

    hours of work and,   4, 5
    inadequate,   6
    incapacity for work and,   4
    Industrial Tribunals and,   6
    information included in,   3-6
    injunctions and,   8
    job description and,   4, 5
    job title in,   4, 5
    layout and,   4-6
    mobility clauses and,   7
    notice and,   4, 5-6
    pensions and,   4, 5
    places of work and,   4, 5
    remuneration in,   3, 5, 9
    requests for,   7
    sex discrimination and,   6
    sick leave and,   4, 5
    signatures of employees on,   9
    temporary employment and,   4
    time limits and,   3
    unfair dismissal and,   6
    Whitley contracts and,   6
    working rules and,   9
Wrongful dismissal,   135